"Every once in a while, a book lands on my desk that I wish I had read when I was in college. The book you now hold in your hands is one of those books. . . . This is theology at its best. It is both pastoral and personal."
—CAROLYN CUSTIS JAMES, AUTHOR OF *MALESTROM* AND *HALF THE CHURCH*, FROM FOREWORD

"Melanie Springer Mock's *Worthy* is so many things: memoir and resource, theological reflection and cultural critique. As a narrator, she is wise, cantankerous, charming. An astute cultural critic, Mock reads the narratives of North American Christianity for the ways in which they give and hinder life, and offers tools for challenging the forces in Christian and secular culture that insist that we are anything less than created—individually, diversely—in the image of God."
—BROMLEIGH MCCLENEGHAN, AUTHOR OF *GOOD CHRISTIAN SEX*

"Melanie Springer Mock's new book, *Worthy*, truly matters. It matters, as Madeleine L'Engle might say, 'cosmically,' as the author tells her own story of untangling her faith from empty or showy religion and affirms that we are all image-bearers of God and are worthy simply because we exist. I love Mock's sensibility (and good sense) and her call to authenticity and love."
—JENNIFER GRANT, AUTHOR OF *WHEN DID EVERYBODY ELSE GET SO OLD?*

"Reading *Worthy* is like sitting down for a cup of coffee with a best friend you didn't know you had. Melanie Springer Mock both affirms the worthiness of every human being as one created in God's image and gently leads her reader to consider larger questions of social justice in the context of individual worth. This book is a must-read for anyone who has ever felt like an outsider, watching the parade of haves go by while perennially feeling like a have-not."
—ELRENA EVANS, EDITOR AT EVANGELICALS FOR SOCIAL ACTION

"When we are truly, deeply loved, the way Jesus loves, our hearts and minds expand beyond all knowing. This book doesn't just describe that love; it takes you inside it through the power of story. Reading these beautiful, vulnerable stories will make you feel worthy in your very bones—and will inspire you to love others the same way. What good news!"
—SHIRLEY HERSHEY SHOWALTER, AUTHOR OF *BLUSH*

"Melanie Springer Mock's *Worthy* uniquely weaves scholarly inquiry and good storytelling into a powerful witness. Through it she touches virtually every area of demeaning and destructive division in modern society and in evangelical Christianity. Her memoir, written in the tradition of spiritual autobiography, helps readers see that Jesus' life and unconditional love have indeed changed 'the sentence structure—and thus the power structure' for all of us, from one of never being enough to one of being profoundly worthy just as we are."
—BETTINA TATE PEDERSEN, PROFESSOR OF LITERATURE AND WOMEN'S STUDIES, POINT LOMA NAZARENE UNIVERSITY

"Using her own life as a flashlight, Melanie Springer Mock wonderfully illustrates ways to discover worth when 'not enough' is the message most often heard in Christian and secular cultures. If you are yearning to be simply and amazingly you in Christ and in community, read this book. It certainly touched me."
—MARYKATE MORSE, AUTHOR AND SPIRITUAL DIRECTOR

WORTHY

WORTHY

*Finding Yourself in a World
Expecting Someone Else*

MELANIE SPRINGER MOCK

**HERALD
PRESS**

Harrisonburg, Virginia

Herald Press
PO Box 866, Harrisonburg, Virginia 22803
www.HeraldPress.com

Library of Congress Cataloging-in-Publication Data
Names: Mock, Melanie Springer, 1968- author.
Title: Worthy : finding yourself in a world expecting someone else / Melanie
    Springer Mock.
Description: Harrisonburg : Herald Press, 2018. | Includes bibliographical
    references.
Identifiers: LCCN 2017052092| ISBN 9781513802541 (pbk. : alk. paper)
| ISBN
    9781513802558 (hardcover : alk. paper)
Subjects: LCSH: Christian women--Religious life. | Self-actualization
    (Psychology) in women. | Self-actualization (Psychology)--Religious
    aspects--Christianity. | Identity (Psychology)--Religious
    aspects--Christianity.
Classification: LCC BV4527 .M565 2018 | DDC 248.4/897--dc23 LC
record available at https://lccn.loc.gov/2017052092

To those who have loved me, just as I am.
You know who you are.

To be yourself in a world that is constantly trying to make you
something else is the greatest accomplishment.

—Ralph Waldo Emerson

CONTENTS

FOREWORD

Every once in a while, a book lands on my desk that I wish I had read when I was in college. The book you now hold in your hands is one of those books.

I doubt that reading Melanie Springer Mock's *Worthy* would have spared me the deep personal struggles I experienced when my own story veered off the script that I, as a woman, had inherited from my family, church, and culture. But it would have been worth a lot to have her company on the journey and to hear her voice of experience in the process.

This book is part memoir, part sage advice—a compelling mix of Mock's own story and the kinds of struggles she's encountered along the way that left her believing she didn't measure up as a Christian, a woman, a mother, and a professor. Her story isn't unique, which is why this book is such a gift. I suspect all readers will find themselves somewhere in the struggles she's experienced.

I was only a few paragraphs into the book when I started seeing my own story in hers. Like Mock, I grew up in Oregon with the expectations that come with being a pastor's kid.

Like her story, mine also veered from the church's "biblical" script for women when, post-college, instead of marriage and motherhood, I entered a long and unexpected stretch of singleness. Marriage didn't recover that script. Instead, I became the family breadwinner in a career I loved while my husband completed his academic training. Like Mock, I too became a working mother, sharing the same sense of isolation and disapproval she describes as she juggled her twin loves: mom to two boys and college professor.

Mock is a lover of narratives and a wonderful storyteller herself. By weaving her own story in and through the issues she addresses, she draws us in to think more deeply about pressures and negative messages that hinder us from embracing our own uniqueness and the stories we are living. And Mock is right there in the struggles with us.

Early in the book, she writes, "I am not a biblical scholar or a theologian." I understand what she means and why that might be good news to readers. But I reject her disclaimer. She may not be a professional theologian, but her down-to-earth theology is what gives this book the kind of relevance we need. This is theology at its best. It is both pastoral and personal. The brand of theology embedded in this book is deeply rooted in real life. It speaks into our own stories and engages the tough questions and self-doubts we all encounter. It gives us courage and hope when life unexpectedly detours into painful circumstances that leave us feeling lost, abandoned, and unworthy. It makes a difference when our feet hit the floor in the morning.

That's what Mock so beautifully pulls off in this vulnerably honest book.

What prevents this book from being merely another attempt to dispel our insecurities and empower us to "live boldly for

Jesus" is this: Mock lodges her assault against unworthiness with a truth that shatters the slightest suggestion that we or our lives don't matter. The heart of her message is the fact that God created his daughters to be God's image-bearers. This is the ultimate antidote to any sense of unworthiness.

Because we are God's image-bearers, God—not our demographics, circumstances, or whatever chapter of our story we happen to be living—defines us. God has blessed us with the highest possible identity, meaning, and purpose, regardless of how others judge us or how our stories are playing out.

I still wish I'd read this book as a college student. Even now it is a saving grace, for those negative messages never stop. Yet no matter what season of life we're in or how convinced we are that we are unworthy, those who read this book will end up standing strong on solid ground. And that alone makes it a worthy read for all of us!

—Carolyn Custis James, international speaker, adjunct faculty at Biblical Theological Seminary, and author of *Half the Church, Malestrom,* and *Finding God in the Margins* (www.carolyncustisjames.com)

INTRODUCTION

The phone call came when I was deep into my bedtime routine. Leaning over a bowl of Life cereal, my nightly snack, I read through the volume of *Encyclopedia Britannica* open in front of me. Although my brother could spend hours poring over the encyclopedias, I saved my own perusing for the cereal ritual. I could only read so much about elephants, or the state of Kansas, or Madame Curie, or my favorite topic—the human body—with the entry's extra-appealing transparent pages that showed the different layers of skin, muscle, and skeleton.

So there I was, eating my cereal and reading the encyclopedia at the kitchen table, when the phone rang. My mom picked up, and after a moment, turned to look at me while she listened to someone unwinding a long narrative. It was about me, I could easily tell, given the way my mom's eyes were fixed on me, her lips pursing tighter as the conversation continued.

I knew there would be trouble. That I would be *in* trouble. But then my mom said, "Thank you for letting me know."

Silence again; the tension in my mom's face intensified.

"Thank you," she said. "Thank you, but I think I won't be doing anything. I have to let Melanie be who she is." And that was that. She said her goodbye, hung up the phone, and came over to kiss the top of my head. Then she left me to finish my cereal.

With that one phone call, my mom pushed back against all the expectations piled up against her and against me. They were expectations built by our small-town Mennonite community, where she lived as a preacher's wife and I lived as a preacher's daughter, and where we were both fed a constant diet of what we should and should not do as relatives of a pastor.

Despite all those expectations—that I wear dresses, that she sing in the choir, that we both submit to the authority of God, the church, the pastor, my father—despite all those things, my mom had told me I should be who I wanted to be. Hers was a message that has lingered with me for decades, first as a quiet thrum beneath my own consciousness that I did not fit in with those around me. As I got older, though, Mom's words have surfaced for me time and again, a resounding reminder that I was uniquely formed in God's image. That God had created me to be all I was meant to be. That I needed to be who God created me to be, even when the world expected me to be someone else.

All this because of overhearing that one conversation in which my mom said *I need to let Melanie be who she is.* . . . *Let Melanie be who she is.* All this because of the serendipity of the evening ritual that placed me near the phone when a grown woman called my mom to tattle.

Earlier that evening, I had been at a quilting bee for middle school girls held in the church fellowship hall. Our group—a Mennonite Girl Scouts of sorts—was called the Loyal Workers.

This name now seems entirely fitting for a collection of Mennonite girls, all learning their place in a culture that privileged hard work and fidelity to God over all else—all else except, on this night, a Christmas party the group leaders wanted us to plan as we sewed quilt blocks.

One of the two loyally working moms offered to host the party, floating the idea that we could have a white elephant gift exchange and taffy pull. Granted, these were innocuous enough activities, but they seemed, to my worker heart, a bit too self-focused.

"I think having a taffy pull is selfish," I said. My friends' needles hovered over the quilt frame, stilled by this moment of insubordination from the preacher's kid—the PK.

"Why are we making taffy for ourselves when we should be helping others?" I said. "We could be caroling at the old folks' home or something. Those people loved it when we caroled there before. Shouldn't we do that again?"

Mrs. Funk's face tightened. "You've all been working so hard," she said. "We'd like to reward you. And besides, other groups will be caroling at the Mennonite home."

This seemed like a lousy excuse, and I said as much. "What are we, loyal workers or loyal loafers?" My older brother had coined that phrase, loyal loafers, and it sounded funny when he used it at home.

But bringing it out at a church meeting was apparently unwise. The conversation was over.

"I think the taffy pull is a great idea," Mrs. Funk said. End of story. My eyes burned, and while I contemplated flipping the entire quilt frame in a pique of anger, I simmered quietly instead, thinking about the crummy taffy pull and how stupid this whole "loyal workers" thing was, anyway.

When Mrs. Funk called my mom later that evening, I fully expected to be disciplined. Pastors' daughters have images to uphold, and clearly I'd once again failed my parents by being mouthy and opinionated, traits that regularly got me in trouble at school too. Instead, my mom gave me a tremendous gift, letting me know I was free to become my own person—to become, in no uncertain terms, exactly who God wanted me to be, despite others' expectations.

And yet.

And yet, for much of my life, I've never truly believed what my mom told me: that I needed to be who I was created to be. Not when I was twelve, or when I was a teenager, or when I was a young adult, a new bride, a struggling mother. Like many others, I've chafed against the expectations established for me while also assuming I needed to be someone else if I wanted to feel loved, affirmed, worthy. For me, a woman growing up in the late twentieth century, these expectations seemed especially pronounced, and I have struggled to reconcile what my culture tells me a Christian woman should be with what I feel called to be as someone created by and loved by God.

Now, nearly one-half century old, I'm finally saying, "Enough." Enough to the messages telling me that I am not enough and that I need to be someone else by virtue of my gender, my age, my body size, my religion. Enough to hearing that if I just changed one aspect of my personhood, I would be worthy. Enough to believing that I am not enough because I haven't conformed to others' expectations for me.

No matter who we are, we all wade against a tide of messages telling us who we ought to be. We hear—from the pulpit and Christian culture, from mass media and our peer groups—that we are not good enough, not disciplined enough, not attractive enough, not strong enough, not pure enough. (And also, not white enough. Not straight enough. Not rich enough. Not normal enough.) These messages are persistent and potent, and they start at a young age. For many of us, such dissatisfaction compels us to believe that if only we could change some aspect of who we are, we could finally be happy, settled, and loved, by others and by God. We will finally have arrived. The self-improvement industry, which brings in $10 billion each year, has as its foundation this sense that we can be far more than we are right now if only we improve our efforts toward transformation. Maybe the next diet, the next job, the next haircut will make us better than we ever were before and more worthy of the space we occupy in this world.

Christians have not been immune to this trend. For those who follow Jesus, the messages about not being enough are sometimes freighted with language suggesting that God disapproves of us being exactly who we are, just as we are. The Christian marketplace is flooded with self-improvement products that have a Jesus-flavored vibe. These are targeted especially at women, who learn "biblical" wisdom about how a warm makeup palette and a colonic cleanse can help them attain the godliness to which they aspire.[1]

No doubt about it—Christian marketers are getting rich on our desire to become more godly and to feel more worthy, and on our sense that our disaffection with life can be eradicated if only we change. A well-worn quote, found nowhere in the Bible but stitched into pillows and slapped onto car bumpers, expresses this sensibility well: "God loves you for who you are, but also too much to leave you that way." Too often, this idea has been used to bludgeon us into change rather than promoting acceptance of how we are created. Despite our best efforts, we do not live up to the expectations demanded of us as women and men, as Christians, as parents, as spouses, as peers. This can lead to self-loathing and the sense that we have not only failed ourselves and others but also failed God.

Imagine what might happen, though, if we learned to push back against those expectations, just as my mother did over thirty years ago when she declared that I needed to be exactly who I was to people who expected someone else. Imagine if we could declare, "I need to be who God created me to be," and if we could feel satisfied in that declaration. Imagine if we could accept who God created us to be, despite the expectations telling us we need to become someone else entirely. Doing so would help us to feel more settled at each moment of our lives. Instead of always assuming the next improvement will bring us joy, we might recognize that the moment is all we really have to be who we are, as we are, and that being in the moment is enough.

That is what this book is about: accepting who God created us to be, even if that acceptance means swimming against expectations that would tell us to be something, or someone, else. It's about acknowledging that we are inherently worthy, no matter who we are, no matter what we do. It's about recognizing that embracing our inherent worthiness is much more than a self-help enterprise; instead, it is part of a justice movement that recognizes every person as an image-bearer of God, already, just as they are.

In the first part of *Worthy*, I explore some of the places where we hear messages about our worth. We are pressured to conform not only by the popular culture we consume but also by the narratives we tell about our lives, by the language we use to define ourselves, and by our church and family traditions.

Living in a world expecting someone else means to be awake and aware of the messages we receive, and the opening chapters of *Worthy* help wake us to influences we might not even recognize or understand. The second section tackles the specific kinds of messages we hear about our worth. Finding ourselves in a world expecting someone else means acknowledging that we are fearfully, wonderfully made, no matter what we hear about gender roles, our embodied selves, the paths our lives take, or what it means to be loved by God. The final chapters of this book celebrate the ways we acknowledge our worthiness—by forging right relationships with others and creating loving communities where all people are included, no matter who they are.

Worthy is a call to accept—and celebrate—the amazing diversity of God's people, as well as a challenge to all the ways the world expects us to be someone else. It goes without saying that this book is neither a call to a heedless embrace of all our worst traits nor the permission to sin boldly. It is also not a self-help book, dispensing advice about how we can love ourselves and each other in three easy steps. I'm not advocating self-fulfillment that comes at significant cost to others, nor a "Be yourself!" ideology that carelessly casts aside those who have stood in your way. *Worthy* instead challenges us to work within the context of our communities. It asks us to mindfully examine the messages we receive and send and to then responsibly and lovingly making space for all of us to be who God has created us to be. In a way, I guess, I want us to be a little like my sweet Mennonite mom, who granted me permission to be my own best self all those years ago.

Much of this book is based on my upbringing in Western Christianity and my continued employment at a Christian college in the evangelical Friends tradition. I realize that other people, having grown up in other cultures, will hear other messages about who they are supposed to be. And I know that for some, expectations can be so much more confining or limiting than they are for me, a fairly privileged white woman living a fairly privileged life. My perspective might seem like a limitation in my analysis of culture—a particular flaw I might have taken care of in therapy rather than through writing a book. Yet through countless conversations with others, with my students, and friends, and kids, and kids' friends, I know I am not alone in believing I am not enough, just as I am. I know I'm not the only one who has spent a lifetime longing to be worthy. Far from it.

I am not a biblical scholar or a theologian, and these pages will not include in-depth exegesis of Scripture. Instead, this book relies on the ways of thinking I use in my work as an English professor, which is perhaps the coolest vocation ever. *Worthy* is shaped by my interests in story, in language, and in the ways we imperfectly use words to figure out life experiences. This book might also be informed, just a little, by my interest in popular culture, and by my belief that cultural artifacts—like Top 40 music, Christian fiction, reality television, and social media—both reflect and shape the world in which we live. It's a world that too often feels fractured, entrenched in divisive thinking that separates us from each other and that dictates who belongs and who does not.

What would happen if we saw our world through the lens of worthiness? What if we could repudiate the voices that demand we become someone other than who we were created to be? The Bible's grand narrative expresses God's love for us. That love—unconditional, unending—is enough of a foundation on which we can stand. The Bible isn't absolutely clear about a lot of things, but Scripture is clear that God models the kind of grace and love we are to extend to each other, without condition.

Matthew reports that the Pharisees, hoping to trap Jesus with their questions, wondered what the greatest commandment was. Jesus responded by saying, "'You shall love the Lord your God with all your heart, and with all your soul, and with all your mind.' This is the greatest and first commandment. And a second is like it: 'You shall love your neighbor as yourself.' On these two commandments hang all the law and the prophets" (Matthew 22:37-40).

We might quibble about what Jesus really means by loving your neighbor and loving yourself. We might disagree about what it looks like to love God with all your heart, soul, and mind. But loving God and loving others means affirming that we are all inherently image-bearers of God; that we are worthy of love, simply because we exist; and that loving others means creating space for God's people to become who God has created them to be.

For a million reasons, I'm grateful for my mom. She gave me life, a comfortable home, and a love for baking. But best of all, she gave me this tremendous gift: the freedom to be my own self. This gift came to me in a small Kansas community, where people sometimes gossiped behind closed doors about that PK who caused all kinds of problems. My mom's love, expressed in her simple response on the phone, reminds me that I am fearfully, wonderfully, uniquely made, even when—especially when—the world expects me to be someone else.

This book is for her, and for every other person in my life who believed I was worthy, just as I am.

Part I

IN A WORLD
EXPECTING
SOMEONE ELSE

1

THIS IS THE WORLD WE LIVE IN

I had an identity crisis over store-bought granola bars. Not those dry ones that feel like gravel in your mouth, but the ones that are almost candy bars, with chocolate chips on the inside and a chocolaty (not to be confused with *chocolate*) coating. My youngest son loved them, and because his doctor had said we needed to feed him anything possible to help him gain weight—to fatten him up, as it were—I let Samuel eat as many of those granola bars as he wanted, whenever he wanted.

At a book group discussion one night, however, I discovered that good mothers made their *own* granola bars, forgoing store-bought treats and their chemical preservatives and wasteful packaging for something far healthier made at home with the nurturing care only a mom could provide. That night, we were discussing Michael Pollan's *Omnivore's Dilemma*, which had been pitched to me as a book wholly undogmatic in its exploration of the food choices we make. This should have been a red flag. Just a few years earlier, someone had recommended a parenting book as being "undogmatic," though I discovered several pages in that because my baby slept in a crib, I was setting him up for a lifetime of criminal behavior. Pollan's book seemed similarly militant about food choices, and I came to the group discussion ready to share some deep eye rolls and snarky comments about the author and about what a poor dinner guest he would be.

But then I discovered that my friends in the book group *liked* what Pollan had written. They wanted to live out his idealism, join community farm associations, give up high-fructose corn syrup. My friends believed we were scarring our children by feeding them cold cereal for breakfast and buying granola bars from the store. By this point in my sons' young lives (they were around five at the time), I knew I'd done enough damage to make therapy a necessity for them when they were adults: I worked outside the home, left them with caregivers, allowed them to watch TV for an hour each day. But I didn't realize I'd been also damaging them by purchasing chocolaty granola bars.

Now I'd heard the truth. If my kids were going to eat granola bars, I needed to make them myself—for the sake of the kids and the entire planet. What else could I do? I spent thirty dollars on ingredients and an afternoon in the kitchen, making granola bars . . . which my kids almost immediately rejected because they weren't chocolaty enough and fell apart in their hands. For the next few weeks, I consumed an entire recipe's worth of those darn bars, which broke apart in my backpack and stained my work files with blobs of sticky oats and raisins. Throwing out the failed experiment was not an option, my frugality compelling me to finish every last unsavory bite.

Maybe Michael Pollan was right, and I needed to at least reconsider the ways I was feeding my family. Maybe my book group was right, and homemade granola bars represented the last frontier in conscientious parenting. At the time, I certainly believed the messages I heard: that unless I changed something as fundamental as where I sourced my granola bars, I was not doing right by my children, my community, my world. I didn't take much time to ask myself if that message was true, because it seemed so pervasive and convincing, especially as it was coupled with other assertions I'd already been hearing, for five years at least, about what good Christian mothers were supposed to be doing. Instead of wondering whether making granola bars was *really* an activity that might make me a better mom, I simply gathered up the materials and began to bake.

In the grand scheme of things, feeling compelled to bake crummy granola bars is not that big a deal. Cumulatively, I was out only thirty bucks and an afternoon's labor. I know that having the resources to make my own food also reflects the extraordinary privilege I enjoy. I have enough space in my life to indulge angst about food choices, plus the money to make decisions about feeding my family free-range chicken, grass-fed beef, and preservative-free granola bars.

Still, this story has been symbolic for me of the many messages I received as a new mother, from both popular and Christian culture, as well as from my home community—messages telling me exactly who I was expected to be as a Christian mother. From the moment my husband and I publicly announced we were expecting our first child, I'd been hearing those messages both explicitly and implicitly: from well-meaning colleagues who wondered when I would be quitting my tenure-track position to take care of my son; from books reminding me that loving mothers carried their babies everywhere, slept with them, and nursed exclusively; from magazine articles suggesting that the baby food we purchased from the store would rot my son's teeth and give him diabetes before high school graduation.

I carried the accumulation of these many messages like a chip on my shoulder. Over time I came to believe that nearly everyone was judging the personal choices my husband and I made for our family—or actually just judging me, because the messages men get about family, children, and work are different from the ones women receive. Perhaps I needed to be more resilient, to challenge the messages I'd been given. But because I wanted to be the best parent possible for our sons—and really, who doesn't want to be the best parent possible?—my resistance to any potential judgment of my mothering skills was quite low.

Facing judgment about my mothering skills is a first-world problem, for sure; others face expectations far more daunting and far more damaging to their sense of worthiness than a silly encounter with granola bars and parental judgment. Yet in ways big and small, we are all swimming in a stew of expectation.

This is the world we live in.

MY VOCATION AS AN ENGLISH PROFESSOR has given me an extraordinary gift: the opportunity to spend my days with young people who are transitioning from childhood to adulthood and who are establishing independence from the parents, churches, and cultures that raised them. While our class time is often given over to journalistic convention and the sweet power of a well-placed semicolon, conversations outside of class turn to my students' attempts to figure out life; they wonder to what vocation they are called, whom they should love and marry, where they should live, and how they are supposed to act as young men and women attending a Christian university. For some, these conversations are especially fraught, because they deal with the essence of students' identities. How are women supposed to have voices when they are told to be silent? How are students of color expected to navigate a university culture that still privileges whiteness? How are LGBT students expected to have any measure of self-esteem when their very being is considered by some peers to be an abomination? How are those living with a mental illness diagnosis expected to navigate the stigmas that come with their disorder? My students want to know how they are expected to be themselves in a world expecting someone else entirely.

Because so many of us grow up deeply committed to watching television and listening to Top 40 radio, it would be easy to assume that popular culture alone is responsible for shaping our sense of self and the deeply entrenched belief that we have never been the people others are expecting us to be. The influence of the Web has put media messages on steroids, and we are constantly bombarded by images telling us exactly who and what we should be, what we should wear, how we should look, whom we should love. As the mother of two teenage boys, I understand the fears some parents have about popular culture's negative influences. Like most of their peers, my kids have cell phones that put all kinds of media at their fingertips, and we've had numerous discussions about limits on what they view, listen to, or post on their smartphones. These conversations with my kids have been the most difficult I've had with them, because, like most teenagers, my sons don't fully realize how damaging media can be. Any limits I put on their pop culture consumption are not so much because I worry about my kids' eternal lives or about Satan speaking to them between the tracks of their latest favorite albums, as Christian parents of my generation feared. Instead, I worry about the way some media can whittle away at their self-esteem. When they are carefully curating every image they send to their friends, and when each selfie is commented on, liked, and shared—or, more disastrously, *not* liked or shared—they might feel that they are not enough, just as they are.

So I know that popular culture conveys all kinds of messages about who we are expected to be, as teenagers, young adults, and middle-aged parents. Most of us are shaped by the mass media we consume. I'd like to believe that because I'm older, wiser, and better educated than I used to be, I have some kind of bulwark protecting me from media influences. But no. I'm well aware that the media continues to shape who I believe I need to be, even as I also know I'm being manipulated. Standing in the grocery line, looking at celebrity magazines, I can simultaneously conclude that the images I see are photoshopped . . . and wish mightily for the glowing skin and toned arms of the beautiful women I see pictured there. How much more convincing such magazine covers are for younger folks, whose critical thinking skills and frontal lobes are not so developed and who see, over and over again, messages about what it means to be not only prized, but also accepted and loved.

Christian popular culture is no less culpable in creating a world of expectations, and sometimes the messages we as Christians embrace are even more rigid in their insistence that people need to conform. As I've studied Christian popular culture for the past half decade, I see so clearly the ways Christian music, books, blogs, magazines, and movies set up expectations for how we are to act as women and men who follow Jesus. Often, though, we are asked to accept these expectations without a second thought, because the messages established by Christian popular culture are packaged as "biblical," and thus beyond reproach. Many Christians are not willing to consider that the creators of Christian popular culture are no less savvy than their seemingly secular counterparts at making a buck. For Christian marketers, however, that money comes in the good name of Jesus.

Regardless of whether popular culture is sacred or secular, we are branded by it, and that imprint often reminds us that we are unworthy unless we consume what we're being offered. While many Christians believe that steering clear of seemingly secular popular culture will protect them—and their children—from inappropriate messages, both Christian and secular popular culture want us to conform: to be different from who we are in order to be accepted, even when that difference looks like everybody else; to wear the right clothes, listen to the right music, buy the right Bible studies, have the right look, and accept the right dogma, packaged in the right biblical language.

No doubt about it, then. We are inundated with messages from mass media, telling us who we should be. Knowing this, it might be advisable to turn off our smartphones, give up our Netflix accounts, get off the grid, and renounce those persistent media messages entirely. Still, I would argue that my steady diet of *Real Housewives* programming, Top 40 ballads, and *People* magazine has only gone so far in shaping expectations for how I should walk through this world. I have also been influenced by my upbringing, by the Christian environment in which now I live and work, and by a Western Christian ethos that has informed broader culture, creating fairly rigid expectations about being a woman—and having a female body—in ways that mass media has never done for me. Those raised in cultures defined by an evangelical Christian ideology learn there are distinct characteristics that make someone worthy of inclusion in the body of Christ—or not worthy. Contemporary Christian culture has done a good job of excluding those who don't fit its "godly" paradigm.

Not all expectations are bad, of course. Both popular and evangelical cultures have, at times, endeavored to create positive messages that provide us with the direction and courage we need to experience a rich life. But even presumably positive messages can have deleterious effects, especially when they are packaged as generalizations applicable to an entire people group. It would be no less damaging to hear that God designed *all* women to be kind and thoughtful, for example, than to be told that all women are, by their very nature, pretty princesses. Both messages dismiss differences between us, and fail to consider the ways we are, each of us, individually designed to be exactly who God distinctly created us each to be.

In recent years, I've started to use specific language to help clarify the issue of rigid expectations and their role in my spiritual journey. That language has helped me see that God created all of us to be our unique selves, and has helped me see that expectations often erase this uniqueness. In finding this language, I am so grateful for a serendipitous encounter with an octogenarian feminist named Letha Dawson Scanzoni. It was her book *All We're Meant to Be*, coauthored with Nancy Hardesty, as well as her mentorship, that gave me the language I needed to understand why pushing against expectation is vital to my life as a Christian. In *All We're Meant to Be*, the authors convincingly show that the Bible, written by men and in patriarchal societies, still tells a compelling story of women acting faithfully as leaders, prophets, and disciples, and that Jesus' ministry intended to liberate all people to fully become image-bearers of the divine.[1]

Being who God created us to be means taking Psalm 139:14 seriously. The psalmist asserts, "I praise you, for I am fearfully and wonderfully made." If we really are fearfully and wonderfully made, we need to stop acting like there's a footnote to the psalmist's assertion, one that says we are fearfully and wonderfully made, *but* . . .

. . . but some differences between us need to be obscured. But some are more wonderfully made than others. But some people have the right to tell others what being fearfully and wonderfully made really looks like. Think about it: our disagreements within the church and without have turned on the assertion that our brothers and sisters are fearfully and wonderfully made, but only if they look and act enough like us so that our differences fade away. When we assert that *all* Christians must act in a certain way, or that *all* women need to relate to others in a specific manner, our own separate identities are blunted. And when we fail to live up to expectations about the way *all* Christians act, we also learn to believe we are not worthy, just as we are.

When I began studying Christian popular culture a half decade ago, I discovered an extended metaphor that seemed especially apt in describing the dissonance that Christian culture tends to create within and between us. I likened this culture to the divisiveness of middle school, where lines were drawn between those who belonged and those who did not. Sometimes those lines in middle school seemed inexplicable, arbitrary: the in-crowd determined by whether one wore Calvin Klein jeans or some cheap knockoff, as if denim itself might deem one person more worthy and more lovable than another. At times, the lines were impenetrable, even if you begged your mom to spend more money than she ever thought reasonable for jeans, and you wore the jeans to school, only to discover that the in-crowd included those with Calvin Klein stamped on their bottoms *and* keenly feathered hair. Those lines were deep, pervasive, damaging. No matter what you did or how you acted, no matter the state of your very own heart, if you were on the outside, you generally remained an outsider, and those on the inside had the prerogative—the God-given right, almost—to treat you poorly. After all, you deserved what-ever treatment you received. You were essentially unlovable. Unworthy. Not enough, just as you were.

Perhaps I resonate with a middle school metaphor because my own adolescence was so miserable and I always felt like an outsider, never worthy enough—never pretty enough, or smart enough, or rich enough—to be accepted by my peers. Or by many of my teachers, for that matter. Being poor and having to wear Kmart clothes was only one part of my struggle, as was my uncontrollably frizzy hair. In middle school, I got to know my principal because of the time I spent in her office as punishment; some teachers had labeled me an "angry teen," which may or may not have been accurate, depending on the day. My anger was fueled in part by being bullied by classmates who mocked my hair and my clothes and my tomboy identity. Their mock-ery included notes passed in hallways, face-to-face insults, and phone calls. Most memorably, during one call, a peer initially acted as a friend but then told me my hair was "[expletive] ugly" and that I really needed to do something about it. In other words, if I wanted to be accepted, I would have to change. Otherwise, I absolutely deserved the condemnation I received.

Most churches, at least, are more delicate in their assertion that folks need to change completely to be made worthy, although this is not always the case, and sometimes we are told that being cast out from a community of faith is a loving response compelling us to change. Such insistence about how every Christian is to be, act, think, and believe produces the same result as those tumultuous middle school years. Either you are as all other Christians or you are not, no matter whether you are trying to be who God created you specifically to be. On the one hand, we hear that God loves us unconditionally and that God's love endures forever (Psalm 136:2); on the other hand, we hear that we must change, must contort ourselves to fit some prescribed box and become like all other believers; otherwise, God will not love us quite so much, and neither will God's followers.

Consider the rhetoric so often used to establish expectations about who Christians are "supposed" to be. Sometimes this language is subtle, yet when a Christian leader says he "speaks from biblical authority," the implication is clear: those who see the Bible differently from the way he sees it have neither any authority nor any clear understanding of the Bible. At times this language is so dismissive that we cannot help but notice its power to set people apart. For example, pastor and author John MacArthur, speaking about how parents should respond to their gay children, suggested that LGBT folks should be alienated, separated from family, isolated, and turned over to Satan. Like others, MacArthur argues that all Christian parents with gay children must act the same way, or else they are not really Christians.[2] (Never mind the gay children who might also be Christian.)

This rhetoric seeks to divide those who fit comfortably into a Christian mold and those who seek a different way of following Jesus. This us-versus-them dynamic exists everywhere in Christian culture: in the sermons given from the pulpit; in the blogs and social networking sites and magazine articles that evangelicals host and write; even in the ways that toys, clothing, jewelry, and other consumer goods are marketed to those longing to be a cool kid who gets to sit with Jesus during lunch and stand by his locker after the final school bell rings. In many ways, Scripture has been profitable, and telling others exactly who they should be is big business. In this, Christian marketers are no different from the mass media that Christians deride for peddling worldliness. Both are asking us to conform to images they manufacture, creating a world that expects us to be someone other than who we are created to be.

For many Christians, *this* is the world we often live in. It's enough to make me give up on Christianity—or at least the church—altogether. But I don't, and for what it's worth, I don't think you should either. There's too much goodness in the world to abandon it completely; too many good people believe the lies they've been told about what they must do to be considered worthy. Those people need us—and we need them—to fulfill that whole "earth as it is in heaven" mandate about which Jesus speaks.

A large part of that mandate requires making popular culture part of our regular diet—because you cannot change what you do not know—and then reminding others, and ourselves, that we are defined not by what we see but by who we are as image-bearers of God. So despite the problematic parts of mass media, I haven't canceled my cell phone plan or taken away my kids' smartphones (at least not on most days!). Instead, I talk frequently with my sons about mindful use of media and questioning popular culture's savvy attempts to buy the images it sells.

I also haven't made plans to abandon the faith, and I hope my children will remain believers into adulthood and recognize what is good and right and just about being a follower of Jesus. Cloistering ourselves from the potentially damaging cultural messages around us won't work, at any rate, because those messages are everywhere, and not just in the popular culture we consume, Christian or otherwise. Messages about our worthiness are embedded in the narratives we tell about our lives. They are woven through the language we use. They are integral to the ways we were raised, for better and for worse.

Messages about our worthiness can even be embedded in a stupid box of granola bars, the chocolaty preservatives conveying to us in a million ways that we are not good enough, just as we are. I know that now. After all, baking granola bars at home does not a godly mother make. My kids will not be more holy because I spent an afternoon trying to live up to some expectations that deserved critique. My snack cupboard trends again toward store-bought granola bars, their soft sweetness a symbol of my attempt to repudiate messages about my worth and to embrace who God created me to be.

2

WHEN BIG JESUS DOESN'T SHOW UP

During high school, my favorite part of every summer was taking the winding road up through Oregon's coastal range to Drift Creek Camp. The church van, a 1970s-era green clunker, navigated the tight curves and gravel washboards poorly. Jammed into the wobbly back seat for the two-hour journey to camp, my church friends and I put ourselves as far away from the uptight driver as possible. By the time we arrived, taking the final downhill swoop into the lodge parking lot, most of us were a little carsick, but giddy too: we'd made it again, to the place that felt like home.

The cabins at Drift Creek were damp, dark, and in some years, a haven for rodents. The bathhouse seemed miles away, and walking through the forested path at night was so frightening that I often dehydrated myself during the day just so I wouldn't have to pee after bedtime. The camp creek was ice-cold, and swimming (in those days, without a lifeguard) was dangerous, as a friend and I discovered when we were at the creek alone, got caught in an eddy, and struggled back to shore. When I was too old to be a camper, I got hired to wash dishes, spending long hours with hands deep in soapy pools of water, scrubbing out giant bowls and pans for about twenty bucks a week.

Despite all this, and despite the cold rain that came with summers near the Oregon coast, Drift Creek Camp was heaven to me. I loved the community I found at Drift Creek—other kids who shared my denominational heritage and who could sing Mennonite hymns without needing to see the words. I also loved the camp counselors, my earliest spiritual role models—especially the cute college boys, who seemed so much older and more mature than I was. Most of all, though, I felt grounded when at Drift Creek. Like a million other kids who have experienced the natural high of church camp, I came home from my summers at Drift Creek recommitted to being a good Christian daughter and sister and friend. That commitment usually lasted a day or two, until a sibling did something really annoying, evoking in me a rage that managed to erase several weeks of church camp nirvana.

In 1982, I decided to be baptized at Drift Creek, not during the summer camp program but while our church was at its yearly retreat—a weekend that was not nearly as fun as regular camp, because my parents and other adults were around and would yell at us kids to be quiet after ten at night. But I loved Drift Creek so much that being baptized there felt like a significant decision.

It was the only decision I made, really, about this important step in my faith life. The whole ritual seemed a matter of course. I was fourteen, the appropriate age for such things. My dad, the church minister, would baptize me. I would be sprinkled with water, rather than dunked, because that's what our church tradition dictated. There would be no Jesus prayer, no asking Jesus into my heart, no public confession of faith. I would read something I'd composed myself, an angsty poem that rhymed *love* and *dove* and *above*. I'd kneel to let my dad pour water over my head, then wait while other adults came forward to give me awkward hugs and handshakes, welcoming me into the fellowship of believers.

When it was over, little had changed. In fact, I'm sure my friends and I spent the rest of that day making fun of the quirky family in our church, our favorite unsanctioned youth group activity.

My baptism experience reflected my particular Mennonite upbringing, the act of believers baptism an important doctrinal distinction that had separated followers of Menno Simons from other church reformers in the sixteenth century, lending these followers the name Anabaptist (*ana* being the Greek term meaning "again," or "re-"). Both my parents were Mennonites—my mom by birth, my dad by choice—and I had been raised in a denomination that emphasized Jesus' ministry, his attention to those on the margins, his teachings on peace and humility. The adults in my life expressed their Christian faith quietly but ardently, and I grew up believing that every other Christian I knew, no matter the denomination, followed the same spiritual trajectory that I had: attending church from birth, getting baptized as a teenager, then going to church some more. Despite sometimes accompanying friends to their churches and spending a week of eighth-grade catechism studying different denominations, I assumed that most of my Christian friends had faith journeys similar to my own. No one disabused me of this notion.

It took growing up, leaving home, and meeting other Christians to recognize that stories about our faith matter, deeply, and that one of the most persistent ways Christian culture establishes expectations for Jesus-followers is by privileging certain narratives about the spiritual journey. This might seem an obvious assertion. Of course stories have tremendous power to shape our understanding of the world; otherwise there would be no need for literature, theater, or even reality television. More than any other writer, Madeleine L'Engle has helped me conceive of the power that stories confer to us, how they help us order the chaotic matter that life gives us. In *The Rock That Is Higher*, L'Engle writes, "Story makes us more alive, more human, more courageous, more loving. Why does anybody tell a story? It does indeed have something to do with faith, faith that the universe has meaning, that our little human lives are not irrelevant, that what we choose or say or do matters, matters cosmically."[1]

I love this notion, because I love stories so much and have spent my teaching career helping my students understand that their own narratives about their own lives matter. Yet despite the immense power we give to stories—the way we affirm that they make us "more human, more courageous, more loving"—we often don't question the ways that predominant stories shape how we understand our own faith journeys.

Which is why, when I was fifteen and at a national Mennonite conference, I boldly answered an altar call. And then, just as boldly, regretted it.

I had traveled to Lehigh, Pennsylvania, for that Mennonite gathering mostly for the cute high school boys and the chance to fly across the country without my parents along to embarrass me. That Tony Campolo was speaking at the conference was a nice bonus to what I knew would be an epic trip. A week without family in a college dorm? Late-night snacks from vending machines? Sign me up! An old-timey revival? I didn't even know what that was.

In the 1980s, Tony Campolo was a hero for Christians and a big name on the Christian conference circuit. He was edgy, dynamic, and would occasionally cuss during his presentations. My parents loved him, so I did too, and family drives in our Chevy Citation often included listening to Campolo sermons on cassette tapes.

What I didn't know was that Campolo was a particular kind of Christian: an evangelical. Nor did I know what being evangelical meant, so the altar call Campolo gave at the national youth conference was my wide-eyed introduction. Campolo delivered a rousing sermon to a room that was crowded and sweltering, filled with young people stewing in the summer humidity. His charismatic speech was electrifying—so much so that when he offered an altar call, imploring us to stand if we wanted to commit our lives to Christ, my first thought was "Why, sure!"

I rose to my feet. But then I looked around, and I noticed that none of my friends were standing. In fact, most people were still sitting—except for me and a handful of others scattered throughout the gymnasium. I couldn't sit back down. Campolo had seen me, had called me out as someone making a life-changing decision. So I stood, and sweated, and waited for Campolo to stop praying already. When he invited those who had stood up for Jesus to come to the front and meet with a spiritual advisor, I slipped away, relieved to have escaped but also still puzzled. Why hadn't my friends stood with me? What had I just witnessed?

Walking back to our dormitory rooms for the night, I was too embarrassed and confused to say anything to my friends. Instead, we talked about the farm boys who were staying in a room nearby and made jokes about the weird girl from our youth group who had decided to feign an ankle injury for the conference week. Poking fun at others had become a cherished activity for me, a way to cover for my own nagging insecurities—about altar calls, my faith, and just about everything else.

A FEW YEARS LATER, when I dove headfirst into evangelical culture as a first-year student at George Fox College, I encountered the phenomenon of an altar call almost weekly during our required chapels. The repetition of this exhortation to commit one's life to Jesus was puzzling to me. Weren't we at a Christian college because most of us were already Christians? What reprobates walked among us, needing to be baptized and welcomed into the family of God?

Plenty, it turns out—at least if you judged from the optional Sunday evening chapel services called Shalom, which I attended mostly out of guilt because others in my dorm went. Although I actually wanted to stay in my room watching TV, I realized that *not* going to Shalom would cause all kinds of conflict with my friend group—so no inner shalom at all, really, not unless I wanted to face my roommates' icy glares and passive-aggressive standing in front of my television set. So I dragged myself to the cafeteria to sing praise choruses I didn't know and to listen while my peers gave their testimonies. This was another evangelical ritual I'd never experienced—not in all my years of Sunday school, vacation Bible school, and church camp. Many of my Christian college peers obviously had, though. When time was allowed during Shalom, they would get up and share their degradation and sin. They'd confess their addictions to drugs and booze and porn; their sexual experimentation in their childhood bedrooms; their descent into Satan's evil lair, until Jesus found them and freed them from sin.

I was astounded. These were the same classmates who led worship, who played guitar in the praise band, and who prayed in small huddles on the campus quad. Had they really been *that* mired in sin? Had Jesus really spoken that vividly to them?

And what exactly was *my* problem? I wondered why this all felt so foreign to me. What was all this big sin of which they spoke? Why had I never been invited to Christian parties where beer flowed freely and the parents' Reliant K car in the garage served as the best place for heavy make-out sessions (second only to a kid's twin bedroom set)? And why had Jesus never—not once!—materialized in front of me, letting me know he loved me, cared for me, had saved me? According to the testimonies I heard during Shalom, Jesus was appearing *all the time*, giving high fives and hugs, emerging from the vapors like Michael Landon in *Highway to Heaven*. What had I been missing all these years, thinking that Jesus and I were already on pretty good terms?

Several years later, while studying conversion narratives in graduate school, it finally dawned on me. I hadn't been missing out, not as far as my faith journey was concerned. Jesus wasn't necessarily boycotting my apartment or limiting his appearances to those with bigger sins to confess. Instead, I began to recognize that the evangelical ritual of giving testimony followed a well-entrenched pattern of the spiritual autobiography, stretching back to Augustine, whose confession launched a tradition of admitting one's gravest sins, encountering the living Christ, and discovering a newly unencumbered self, one free from the sin. There was power in that tradition, to be sure. In different points throughout history, giving testimony was an important way for people to describe God's presence in their lives. Giving testimony knit together faith communities and became an important evangelizing tool, drawing others to Christianity by showing what a life made new in Jesus might look like.

Studying these early conversion narratives, I had new appreciation for the ritual of giving testimony, for its deep roots in American literature, and for the power of story to change lives completely. But I also had an epiphany about how ostracized I had felt at an evangelical college because I lacked a cool testimony to share. I realized that giving testimony, along with the other stories we tell about our faith, establishes expectations that sometimes distort our understanding of Jesus, salvation, faith, and belief.

By the time I had this epiphany, however, it was too late. The expectations about having a great conversion story had already compelled me to lie, and in the boldest way possible.

WHEN, AS AN UNDERGRADUATE, I was asked to share my conversion story, I panicked. Giving testimony had become part of our weekly devotions for the college cross-country team, so I knew my time was coming. But I also knew my boring story—about going to church almost every week of my young life, about being baptized at Drift Creek, about having few big sins to confess—wouldn't live up to expectations. I had to do something to save face.

Since my life didn't conform to the patterns of a conversion narrative, I changed my life a little here and there to meet the expectations that had been in put in place for me. The story I told was a good one, and included the largest sins I could imagine: drinking, carousing, staying out past curfew. My salvation moment came in the form of a high school cross-country coach who pulled me from the brink and turned me back toward goodness and light. Judging by the hugs I received from teammates after I finished, my story succeeded big time, even if those hugs were no less awkward than the ones my church family had given me when I was baptized several years earlier.

What I hadn't told my audience was this: my testimony was knit together by a tapestry of lies, lies based on what I believed others expected from me and from my faith journey. The one or two sips Grandpa had given me from his Schlitz beer can made me nowhere near the alcoholic I claimed to be. I only remember one night of carousing past curfew, but I had tearfully called my mom at three in the morning, wanting to come home. My cross-country coach was indeed an inspiring man, but he was not the Jesus figure my conversion narrative had created him to be. Ironically, my story also didn't make room for what I believed to be the most sizable sins of my youth: my envy, the disrespect I often showed my mom, and the tendency I had to make fun of those deemed weaker than me, including that awkward family at church about whom my friends and I liked to gossip.

But those kinds of sins don't have much purchase when we're talking about our faith journeys, do they? It doesn't seem too miraculous for Jesus to redeem those who dabble in minor sins like envy and gossip. People who have been saved from the grip of substance abuse or sexual addiction? That would take a *real* savior, for sure.

I'M BACK AT GEORGE FOX UNIVERSITY NOW, this time as a professor: back in evangelical culture, back in the place where altar calls and giving testimony are still part of student life, as common as guitar players in the quad and bare-foot undergraduates making out in the campus rose garden. In a memoir class I teach, I like to share my experience of hearing conversion stories for the first time and the shock I felt when I realized nearly everyone around me had not only led lives of degradation and sin but also encountered a Jesus so vibrant and present that it was like he was dropping by the dormitories during coed visiting hours. I also tell my students about my fabricated faith journey, the one I embellished and for which I received warm embraces.

This is the power of stories we tell about our faith journeys, I remind my students. We start to expect that every faith jour-ney should follow a similar trajectory, should look exactly like a three-act play, with the life of sin covered in act 1, the conver-sion in act 2, and the happily-ever-after with Jesus before the curtains go down in act 3. Without a doubt, the stories we tell about our faith journeys set up expectations for others about what being a Christian must look like. Those who have no exciting sins to confess and no big Jesus moments to describe may begin to question whether they are living the right Chris-tian life at all.

So our faith stories can create overwhelming expectations for people, especially when we covet one kind of conversion narrative over all others. And let's face it: Christians love a good salvation story, the kind that shows a sinner's slide into darkness, followed by a shocking Damascus road moment and the promise of being redeemed, then afterward living a perfect life in Christ.

Wonder if this is actually true? Consider for a moment the types of spiritual memoirs regularly published as authentic stories of faith and promoted as exemplars for what the "Christian walk" should look like. Writing for CNN, religion editor Daniel Burke acknowledges as much. His article "The Dirty Little Secret about Religious Conversion Stories" suggests that religious testimonies are, in many ways, like advertisements for weight-loss programs or products. Both rely on closely edited "before" and "after" images, the one standing in dramatic relief to the other. For Christians, Burke writes, the "before pictures, in particular, tend to darken. The snares of sin sharpen, the descent into depravity deepens."[2]

The same pattern of a deep slide into depravity, followed by a miraculous recovery, appears in most contemporary spiritual memoirs. Indeed, this pattern seems crucial to the success of religious memoirs published in the last few decades. If you look at the writers who have gained notoriety for their conversion stories, a similar thread runs through them: the writers were once lost in the mire of Big Sin—substance abuse, pornography, infidelity—but through some miraculous epiphany, they've found new life. The stories we tell about our faith thus tend to sound pretty similar. Nadia Bolz-Weber's *Pastrix* seems a lot like Donald Miller's *Blue Like Jazz*, which is in many ways like Anne Lamott's *Traveling Mercies*. Glennon Doyle Melton's *Carry On, Warrior* and *Love Warrior* are almost a Big Sin mash-up, with substance abuse, pornography, *and* infidelity as the trifecta of degradation from which Melton is ultimately saved. For those giving public testimonies, this pattern becomes a narrative guide, telling people exactly how their faith story should look if it is to be sanctified.

So here's the thing. The stories we tell about our faith absolutely set up expectations about what a Christian life will look like, and those whose lives don't conform to the normal patterns of conversion narratives often feel like outsiders, their relationship to God and to others insubstantial when compared to those who have felt, seen, and heard a living Christ. Telling my Christian college students about my fabricated conversion story, I often see nods of recognition from those who have spent their young lives feeling sheepish about a spiritual journey short on significant trials and long on Sunday nights singing praise choruses with their youth groups. Like me, some might have given in to the temptation to embellish their stories to meet the expectations about salvation we've created. Some might have decided their stories aren't worth telling at all, given the lack of vivid sins and the absence of a larger-than-life conversion that we've come to expect.

The reality is that the conversion stories we tell often compel us to understand our entire faith in a different way. Narratives that turn on one crucial moment when people encounter Jesus make us less likely to see the many other and far more subtle ways we experience Jesus every day: through our interactions with family, friends, coworkers, and church members, and even through the passing connection we make with a stranger sitting at the next table in a coffee shop. Quakers insist that we all have the light of Christ in us, a perspective that acknowledges the ways Jesus is present to us, and within us, moment by moment throughout each day. And yet the conversion narratives we tell each other honor the "Damascus road" type of experience more than any other kind. These types of narratives establish the expectation that meeting Christ had best be monumental and transformative if it is to be *real*, and that Jesus is to be encountered as an outside figure, a completely foreign other.

As someone who did not grow up giving testimony, I had different expectations about my relationship to Jesus and the church. Perhaps that's why I was so confused by Tony Campolo's altar call. When he suggested that we stand up and commit our lives to Jesus, I thought that *of course* Christian young people should be making such a commitment. I mean, who could argue with it? It only took that encounter with an evangelical minister (an experience reinforced by nearly every other religious encounter I had when attending a Christian college) to change my sense about what should happen to me as a believer—and what was not happening, since Big Jesus had never made the same kind of appearance to me.

Once, in a moment of courage during track team devotions, I suggested that a woman who had been hanging around the athletic complex might be embodying Jesus. She was homeless and somewhat annoying, but clearly in need of not only housing but also human connection. I may have been too idealistic then, but I described how convicted I felt that this woman was Jesus, and that we needed to respond more compassionately to her. My observation was quickly denounced. There was nothing that could be done to help her, someone said. She just needed to move on. We were being friendly enough, someone said; why, someone had even witnessed to her. At a time when I was trying to figure out exactly what it meant to follow Jesus, I heard again, emphatically, that Jesus was not present to us in such quotidian ways, and that my lack of a Big Jesus Moment meant my own spiritual life was flawed. I spent the rest of that day's devotional time crying, and I quickly learned never to make such observations publicly again.

In *Traveling Mercies*, Anne Lamott opens with a section titled "Overture" that follows the typical pattern of a spiritual autobiography. The trajectory of her life is similar to other conversion narratives, as the story's dramatic arc details a long and painful slide into darkness and degradation. She is an alcoholic, a bulimic, and a drug user, and she has sex with married men. The overture turns on her moment of finding Jesus hunkered in the corner of her bedroom, present there right after she's had a painful abortion and is hemorrhaging. A catlike figure begins to follow Lamott around her houseboat, a presence she believes is Jesus. In what might be the most unorthodox salvation moment ever recorded, Lamott invites Jesus into her heart by cursing and saying "I quit. You can come in."

What makes Lamott's *Traveling Mercies* unique is not this expletive-laced Jesus prayer but everything else in her book. The subsequent essays detail smaller moments in Lamott's life that are still shot through with grace, reflecting Lamott's continued struggle with sin and the presence of Jesus in her day-to-day encounters. *Traveling Mercies* includes essays on her encounter with a hairy man on the beach, the panic she feels while flying through turbulence, an argument she had with her son on Ash Wednesday, and her inability to love her middle-aged thighs. In each of these essays, she describes conflicts that are replicated in every believer's life: the need to extend grace to others and to ourselves; the ways we continually sin, despite our longing to do and be better; the acknowledgment that Jesus incarnates himself, moment by moment, in the people around us. This kind of narrative, in which we are consistently brought down by our own pedantic sins, seems far more true to life than the conversion stories that have great traction among Christians.

Many of us are resistant to any other faith narrative but the one that offers us big sins, big conversions, and a big life after Jesus has met us in a really big way. Giving *Traveling Mercies* to an older relative as a Christmas gift one year reminded me of this resistance (and also served as a reminder to vet books carefully before giving them as gifts). Sometime later, in January, I asked whether my relative had enjoyed Lamott's book. She reported that no, she had *not* liked *Traveling Mercies* and wanted, in fact, to return the book to me.

Now, I don't mind people disliking my favorite author's work—it's one of the occupational hazards of being an English professor—but the reason she wanted to return Lamott's book was because the essays did not confirm her sense of what a conversion narrative should be. After Lamott was born again, I was told, she should have ceased her sinful ways. She should have stopped using the F-word, and stopped criticizing people, and stopped having sex outside of marriage. What I saw as the brilliance of Lamott's book—that she continued to sin and was repeatedly in need of God's grace—my relative considered to be a severe limitation.

Whether we've said the Jesus prayer or not, been dunked or sprinkled in baptism, been suddenly and dramatically saved or experienced faith as a moment-to-moment decision: no matter what, we will continue to struggle, face difficulty, succumb to temptation. To suggest otherwise—that we are made perfect and infallible by one conversion moment—sets us all up to fail.

Because here's the other problem with the standard conversion narrative: it conditions us to assume all we need is that One Moment to be freed forever from whatever ails us, and that no other intervention is needed. If only that could be the case! I think about my friends who struggle with substance abuse, who long to be freed from the entanglement of their addictions, and who have dedicated their lives to Jesus . . . but who must still do the hard work of recovery and who must fight every single day to resist drinking alcohol, taking prescription drugs, starving themselves, or purging. Sometimes people accept Jesus, renounce their addictions, and live clean and sober forever after. Sometimes they accept Jesus, renounce their addictions, and still struggle. By telling faith stories that turn on this miraculous moment of healing, we convey that things like addiction are sins to be gotten over quickly rather than illnesses that need to be treated.

And really, it's the other Jesus this world needs. Not the miraculous Jesus, saving us with one sweep of his hands, but the Jesus who bends down into the nitty-gritty of the world. Pastor John Pavlovitz writes that Christians "don't need the *walk the aisle, say a prayer, and get out of Hell* kind of Jesus. That Jesus is too easy. That Jesus requires no further work. That Jesus is convenient and accommodating to their lifestyle. That Jesus allows them to leave no differently than when he arrived. That Jesus serves them salvation on a silver platter and asks nothing in return." The real Jesus, the one we need, Pavlovitz says, is the one who requires us to work hard, to reach the marginalized, to live among the poor, to sacrifice our lives for others. Pavlovitz continues: "Jesus did far more than simply give an altar call and stamp sinners for Heaven. If he hadn't, the Gospels would be far shorter and simpler. Instead, they give us an expansive, complex, explicitly beautiful picture of the way we are to live this life."[3]

Our traditional conversion narratives, with their miraculous Jesus moment, the point when people are healed from all transgressions, make no quarter for those who find Jesus, receive grace, and continue to battle their demons. Were it *that* simple,

I suppose, we might not have need for therapists, recovery groups, or even the church itself. The church is a place where we sinners all should be able to gather and find acceptance and peace, no matter what our faith journeys look like and no matter what stories we tell about the road we're still on.

ON THE FIRST DAY of my creative nonfiction class, I ask my students to narrate the most important experience in their (mostly young) lives. After more than a decade of teaching the course, I can easily predict what most of these students will write. Their narratives start with apologies about how uninteresting their lives have been and how they lack unique perspectives. Some of them wonder why they are even taking a memoir class, given that they have no material about which to write. Sometimes they express concern for the semester, especially the syllabus requirements outlining daunting demands to write about their own lives. Although many are technological natives who have spent much of the last decade oversharing on social media, my students tend to believe there's little material in their lives worth exploring through the written word.

And then. After that apology or caveat, they often write the most interesting narratives imaginable. They write about family conflicts, trips with grandparents, their sports achievements, the loss of a beloved pet, or, for one student, what it's like to bring a herd of dairy goats to college.

What I love so much about this course is that by the semester's end, students have discovered that their stories do indeed matter, and that even the most seemingly sedate lives can be rich with writing material. Throughout the course, we practice the art of observation, learning to find in each ordinary moment, each ordinary encounter with another person, the extraordinary. Using a series of activities, I encourage students to catalog their commonplace activities, becoming what the novelist Bret Lott calls "explorers of the self," finding beauty and grace in the ephemera of daily living.[4] And then, in almost every class, I ask my students to share what they've discovered with each other. This is not so that they can be critiqued or their grammar and mechanical abilities scrutinized but so that we can celebrate as a community the wonderful world of which we are a small part. By creating space for students to write their own story, apart from expectations about what a "good" story should look like, I hope students will see more clearly the ways they encounter Jesus every single day and are transformed. My students' writing bears witness to these encounters, and to the freedom that accompanies honoring each person's individual story as something worthy, as something that reflects the living Christ.

I sometimes think I teach students less about writing creative nonfiction and more about being aware. I try to teach them to observe the extraordinary in what might seem ordinary lives and surroundings. My students learn, I hope, that they are fearfully, wonderfully, uniquely made, and that what they write—about faith and about other things—reflects God's distinctive imprint on their lives. If I teach them anything during the sixteen weeks we have together, I want them to know that their stories matter because their stories celebrate the Creator, who is at work in each of our lives. Their stories testify to the grace we all need and receive, moment by moment, as we seek to become who God created us to be. I want them to know that their stories—and their lives—are worthy.

If you hear that your story is worthy and that you should tell your story proudly, however seemingly uneventful that story might seem, you might begin to believe your life's journey is remarkable. If you hear that your story bears witness to the unique ways you have encountered Jesus, you might just decide that your story matters and that your faith journey is actually unlike any other. You might decide that your story—even if it lacks one momentous encounter with Jesus—still manifests the many smaller ways Jesus comes to you, moves through, lives in you. Knowing this, you might decide to proclaim your story boldly, rather than embellishing its details the way some undergraduate did nearly thirty years ago. You might come to believe that your story is acceptable—even amazing—just the way it is.

In fact, when you discover that your story matters, you might be willing to express the wonder of it all: Of having been born and raised in the church. Of that day when you felt the water pour down over your head, welcoming you into the fellowship of believers. Of that beautiful moment when you looked up and saw a congregation smiling at you, there in the chapel of the Christian camp you loved, where every summer you were also reborn.

3

STICKY FAITH OR BEING STUCK?

My friend Staci is pretty amazing. I know I may be biased in this assessment—Staci is my friend, after all—but what she's done to reach folks whom Christians might call the "unchurched" is definitely noteworthy, even if few people outside her community have noticed.

In 2011, Staci began working at the Tigard United Methodist Church, in Tigard, Oregon, where her vision of an ecumenical coffee shop took root. Jubilatte opened in November 2011, and for the past six years, Staci has served as a pastorista (pastor + barista), heading a group of volunteers who make lattes and mochas for the parents dropping kids off at the preschool located in the church building, for church members meeting at the coffeehouse, and for people in Tigard stopping by for good drinks and pastries.

Jubilatte might sound like one of those hipster coffee spots embedded in your nearby megachurch—you know, where members praise Jesus with one hand held high, the other hand gripping a Starbucks to-go cup. But what Staci does in her church is so much more than steaming milk into Portland Roasting blends. The motto of Jubilatte is "Conversation not conversion," and Staci has made every effort to ensure that those gathering at the coffeehouse feel welcomed and that they know that their questions about faith are encouraged. For Staci, there are no rigid answers about what it means to be a Christian. Her willingness to foster conversation among those with differing viewpoints has made Jubilatte a warm, welcoming place.

Staci leads book group discussions with people from a variety of church backgrounds. Once a month she also hosts an interfaith gathering, where Methodists and Mennonites sit down to coffee with Mormons and Muslims, with a few Baha'is, Jews, atheists, and Lutherans in the mix. These interfaith meetings have been especially rewarding, and as a regular attender, I've grown a much richer understanding of how those with different faiths navigate the world. My friend finesses these conversations without holding tightly to any one dogma, believing that Christians have much to learn from those who walk another way. What I admire most about Staci is her ability to foster vulnerability during these discussions, and her willingness to be vulnerable by admitting that she holds few answers about very difficult faith questions. In her mind, she has been called to ask questions rather than state firm truths.

At times, however, Staci's far more dogmatic upbringing in a strict fundamentalist home messes with her mind. After several years in seminary and another few decades in ministry, one might think the rough edges of the rigid teaching from her childhood would be rubbed smooth, if not ground to dust completely. But when she talks about the nature of God, Jesus' life on earth, or the inerrancy of the Bible, she remembers what she learned in Sunday school growing up. She knows that what she believes now is good and right, yet she retains a niggling feeling that the theology of her childhood—its inflexibility, its piety, its judgment—would insist that her rich, thoughtful, deep understanding of God is not authentic or real. Even though Staci enacts her Christian faith more authentically than many others I know, she sometimes questions whether she can proclaim that identity at all, given what her upbringing taught her.

Staci and I have talked often about this during long morning runs through the hills around Newberg. Like so many others who have changed their perspective about faith over the span of their adult lives, Staci has landed on what might be labeled a progressive Christian theology, one that focuses on the Gospels and the justice work Jesus did during his time on earth, while also honoring other religious traditions. I understand exactly where Staci is coming from when she expresses a complicated relationship with her religious upbringing. Even though I have faith that God welcomes my questioning and doubts, I sometimes fret in some small corner of my heart that God might smack me down for my lack of trust.

That's one outcome of having deep roots in the faith traditions of our childhoods while also branching out into other ways of knowing and understanding God. It can be difficult to extricate ourselves from expectations for how faith works and how we are to walk through the world. Still, there's a lot to be said for setting down roots in a community, faith-related or otherwise. Roots allow us to feel connected, and they can give us sustenance that helps us grow beyond what we might have imagined. I'm grateful for the deep roots my upbringing gave me and for the ways I've felt attached to a faith tradition and its people.

And yet I sometimes think our familial and community roots have, for too many of us, created a world of intense expectation, insisting we become someone different from who we feel called to be. Perhaps because we care so much about our families and communities and because we don't ever want to let them down, we feel their expectations more assuredly than most anything else. My roots have at times kept me too close to the ground, making me feel that I had to live up to expectations established by my family, my church tradition, my community. Even when those roots have been life-giving, they have also kept me from fully being the unique person I was created to be. Like my friend Staci, tethered still by her childhood religious convictions even when she has tried to break free, I know how our familial expectations and the expectations of our faith communities can anchor us or trap us, can be an instrument of our flourishing or can bind us to roles and ideologies that make us feel less than worthy.

ONLY A FEW MEMORIES STAND OUT from my first week in Hillsboro, Kansas, where my family moved from a Chicago suburb when I was eight. We pulled into the parsonage driveway on an unseasonably warm February day when the schoolkids hadn't been let out yet. Church folks were scrambling through the big, old, beautiful house, putting finishing touches on décor and settling our furniture into its rightful places. Needing something to occupy my time, I walked two blocks uptown to Ray's Supermarket, where an older grocer, no doubt Ray himself, placed me immediately.

"Hey, you must be the new preacher's son, huh?" he said. I was surprised he knew who my family was. I answered in the affirmative—not correcting his misidentification of my gender—and he welcomed me to town. I felt almost immediately that I belonged in Hillsboro, a feeling intensified after I brought home my purchase: a packet of Kool-Aid, the first product I'd ever bought independently of my parents. In my brand-new, hundred-year-old kitchen, I assembled my drink, failing to add sugar. You don't soon forget your first drink of Kool-Aid without any sweetener.

On the second day in Hillsboro, my first at the elementary school, a boy named Shannon intentionally tripped me at recess, and several other kids laughed. Turns out third-grade kids can be far less welcoming than an aging grocer. Being the new girl (or boy—they weren't all sure) wasn't easy. I'd like to say the bullying stopped after that, but it didn't. Kids can be unbelievably cruel, and because I stood out as a preacher's daughter—and especially as a preacher's daughter who looked like a boy—I faced more than my fair share of taunts. There were a few moments when the bullying turned physical. One boy liked throwing rocks at me; another enjoyed covert shoves on the playground. Sometimes kids teased me in class until I cried and then teased me because of my tears.

Yet I remember the five-plus years my family spent in Hillsboro as the best, most formative of my life. The big, airy parsonage was like a cocoon for me, as was First Mennonite, where I started to really learn what it meant to be a follower of Jesus. Even though Sunday school was always boring and I passed many Sundays throwing paper airplanes out classroom windows while my teachers droned on, I know now the religious instruction was vital to my spiritual journey. The older men and women in the church modeled Jesus' love for me in ways I still find compelling. Back in those days, we went to church twice on Sundays and again on Wednesday evenings. Yet I don't ever remember dreading that kind of commitment, probably because the kids all played Ghost in the Graveyard in the parking lot while our parents visited in the fellowship hall after church. My time at First Mennonite was a kind of idyll, the church and its people full of warmth and light.

During our time in Hillsboro, I felt the expectations foisted on me as a preacher's kid much more acutely than I did the expectations for what it meant to be Mennonite. Those expectations were everywhere, probably because nearly everyone knew I was a PK. My public school classmates reminded me often what I could do or say by virtue of my dad's occupation. If I failed to censor myself, someone would tell me I couldn't speak that way because I was a PK. One time in gym I called a classmate a "wuss," and the basketball game stopped, everyone looking at me. "You can't say *that*," one kid said. "Do you even know what that means?" "Of course I know what it means!" I wanted to scream. Instead, I apologized. More than anything else, my mouth got me in trouble, and talking back to teachers gave me consistent access to the principal's office, where Mrs. Jost essentially told me "You can't say that!" over and over again.

Expectations at church were even more rigid, and my clothing choices especially deserved scrutiny. In the fourth grade, when I started wearing culottes to church—part of a green corduroy outfit my mom sewed for me—it was as if I'd caused a major denominational rift. Several friends' mothers called mine, demanding that my mom not let her daughter wear such an outfit to church. It was a slippery slope from culottes to pants, they argued, and their daughters would not be taking *that* nefarious road. In this as well, my mom let me be who I was: a culottes-wearing, loud-mouthed, troublemaking PK.

We moved to a new town two thousand miles away right before I started high school. Our new church in Oregon was far more conservative and, in my mind, far less welcoming than the one in which I grew up. Moving to a new town right before high school inspired me to be a different student, just like the plotline of an after-school special. I promised myself I would be more girlish and less vocal than I had been before. I managed to keep my identity as a PK on the down-low, answering questions about what my father did for a living by lying ("He's a teacher") or simply feigning ignorance ("I'm not sure exactly what he does"). Not having any expectations weighing on me as the PK helped, and people didn't automatically presume how I should act or what I should say. Rumors about my dad's true vocation spread halfway through my sophomore year, however. Playing billiards at a pizza parlor one evening during a basketball team party, I stopped up short when my coach joked that a PK shouldn't be playing pool. The jig was up, and expectations about who I should be as a PK dogged me in high school too.

Despite wanting to shake my identity as a PK, the roots I'd developed in Hillsboro, Kansas, ran deep, and while I chafed against expectations for what it meant to be a PK, I embraced expectations about what it meant to be Mennonite. Those expectations shaped how I was to act as a believer and defined the ways I related to peers who had no church background, as well as to those whose Christian upbringing was entirely different from my own. But in Albany, Oregon, few people knew what it meant to be Mennonite. Sometimes people confused me with Mormons or with the Amish. At those moments, I was compelled to articulate exactly who I understood Mennonites to be. I did so with pride, figuring that the Mennonites had gotten things right and that the Mennonite belief system was beyond reproach. I was well into college before I realized that not all Christians were pacifists, nonconformists, and interested in the separation of church and state. These were tenets of my Mennonite faith that I'd learned while in Hillsboro, even if I didn't understand clearly the theological reasons foundational to those tenets.

That religious education would come much later, when I wrote my doctoral dissertation on Mennonite conscientious objectors in the Great War. For the very first time, I understood the scriptural support for my most ardent beliefs, as well as the church history that had only been hinted at in my childhood. Discovering more about the roots of my faith tradition only enhanced my fidelity to Mennonites and my confidence that Anabaptist theology aligned well with the parts of Jesus' ministry I found compelling.

At times in my life, I've tried on other Christian traditions: a year or two as an Episcopalian and a few as a Methodist, a few months in college as a charismatic Christian, the hand-raising and dancing a fascinating departure from the staid Mennonite services of my childhood. For the last twenty years I have attended an evangelical Friends church, mostly for geography's sake. Even though I've been a member of other denominations for over half my life, the Mennonites still have me. When people ask me how I identify denominationally, I always say I am Mennonite. At my very core, I believe what I learned growing up about Christianity, and I try to practice the religious disciplines central to my faith.

My religious roots run deep and sustain me.

For some people, this is not the case, and the expectations about how they were to act as Christians seem so rigid and dogmatic that they have rejected the faith of their childhoods completely. Many Christians—contemporary and otherwise— have an unfortunate tendency to establish rules for how all believers should act and then to ostracize those who fail to measure up to those expectations. Rather than believing—really believing—that God's grace extends to all, too many Christians decide that those who do not meet certain litmus tests for behavior need to change, and cannot be in the community of the faithful until those transformations are complete. The Bible is used as a winnowing tool, with those claiming biblical authority deciding who belongs and who remains on the outside, even as others find in the Bible counterevidence that suggests a more inclusive understanding of Jesus and his ministry.

A Pew study published in 2015 shows a decline in church membership, especially among millennials (according to the Pew study, those born between 1981 and 1996); a full 35 percent of millennials define themselves as having no religious affiliation.[1] In postmortems of the Pew survey, several writers and thinkers hypothesized that the "nones" were leaving the church because it had become too exclusive.[2] For some people, the insistence on conforming to one vision of faithfulness is problematic, and rather than fit into an inflexible mold the church has created, they have decided to abandon church altogether. Thanks in part to the Internet and social media, younger generations live in a world that views differences more positively. They have an expansive understanding of Christianity, one that does not so rigidly establish rules and expectations for how people are to act, speak, live.

In an article shared widely on social media, author Rachel Held Evans articulated well the reasons why millennials are abandoning their religious roots:

We want an end to the culture wars. We want a truce between science and faith. We want to be known for what we stand for, not what we are against.

We want to ask questions that don't have predetermined answers.

We want churches that emphasize an allegiance to the kingdom of God over an allegiance to a single political party or a single nation.

We want our LGBT friends to feel truly welcome in our faith communities.

We want to be challenged to live lives of holiness, not only when it comes to sex, but also when it comes to living simply, caring for the poor and oppressed, pursuing reconciliation, engaging in creation care and becoming peacemakers.[3]

This vision of the church is not limited to millennials, of course, although it *does* suggest a break from the religious roots that many share: roots that have created a Christian world with a rigid sense of what people of faith should be like. And while many millennials are breaking from the church altogether, there are other ways to contend with Christian traditions that seems too limiting, too divisive: that is, to remake the church from within, doing the hard work necessary to let others know that all are worthy of sitting at God's expansive table, just as they are.

AS A PARENT, I've been told often that I should aspire to teach my children a faith similar to my own—to help my kids set down similar roots, as it were. Christian education is intent on helping kids develop the faith of their fathers and mothers, and countless books offer parenting advice about how we can successfully provide spiritual formation for our children.

Christians are compelled to teach their children some kind of "sticky faith": that is, a faith that will stick with them even into adulthood and that replicates the sincerity and devotion of their parents.[4]

Despite the deep religious roots my own parents gave me, I have resisted this notion. Perhaps I'm just too cynical these days; perhaps I've seen too many Sunday school curricula that seemed more like indoctrination than guidance. With my children, part of the problem is that my faith is different from their father's; he is much more theologically conservative than am I, and his religious roots spring from an entirely different branch of Christianity. Teaching our children the "faith of their parents" can sometimes seem a losing proposition, as I'm sure it must be for many families in which differences exist. But part of the problem is also that I want my children to step outside of the expectations my own faith has set for me and to discover for themselves what it means to be a thinking, questioning Christian. I want them to grow their own strong roots, roots that allow them to be who God created each of them to be, separate from their parents and our beliefs.

Yet this is not the message we often hear. Our hymns and anthems celebrate a faith that passes along the same messages and dogma; we wring our hands when our children choose a different path in their faith journeys. My father even did this, when I tried being charismatic for a turn. When I told him about the exciting new church I'd been attending, he expressed disapproval, not wanting his daughter to get in too deep with the Holy Rollers. But insisting that younger generations take on the faith of their fathers and mothers conveys to them that their individuated belief systems are not good enough, and that conforming to a singular version of Christianity is not only expected but necessary for those who follow Jesus. No wonder so many denominations are splintering, and often along generational fault lines. Churches that require their young people to take on the same exact worldview as their mothers and fathers, who fear questions and resist doubts, are diminishing the differences that exist between us all—differences that, when muted, keep us from being the truly dynamic people of faith we could be.

Although the image is entirely too cliché, I find the metaphor of deep roots and tall trees a good one when I think about the expectations our faith traditions can give us. Several towering oak trees dot the green space beside my office building, named Minthorn Hall. The trees are lovely to look at, especially in summertime when their shade keeps my ancient, un-air-conditioned office coolish. But in winter, when strong winds buffet the campus, I tell my students to run fast into Minthorn, because at times giant branches have broken off from the trees, crashing to the ground. In the last decade, at least three trees have fallen on the quad, and although there were people around to hear them crash, thankfully no one was hurt. Turns out that for several decades, the quad has been overwatered. While this has created a lush green lawn, an inviting one on a warm spring day, the overwatering has killed the roots of the trees, making them appear strong even when they have no foundation. Contrary to their appearance, they are weak, literally rotten at the core.

Other than being legitimately frightened of the trees in windstorms, I have also found these trees to be an important metaphor for me of what rigid religious expectations can do to us. Being told exactly what we are to believe can weaken our roots, making it harder for us to stand on our own, especially when we are battered by life's challenges. Instead of assuming that everyone should conform to a singular expression of faith, we should all be fostering deep, vibrant roots that help people grow strong in their own ways. Only when we are able to do that will we believe that we are worthy, that our faith journey is enough, just as it is. We will learn that it is okay to say something surprising, or different, or even heretical once in a while. Raising questions and doubts about faith does not mean we are doomed; allowing others, including children, to ask good questions about their religious wanderings and wonderings does not mean they will abandon the deep roots of their faith. Instead, our diverse religious journeys can make us stronger, serving like those tangled roots beneath a forest path that keep every tree standing.

It might seem from what I've written that my parents were pretty near perfect with regard to my faith education, or that it was only my dad's position as a pastor that exerted negative religious pressure. By luck or by intention, my parents did foster in me a healthy willingness to explore what it meant to be a believer without the attendant expectations to be or act a certain way. In many ways, given the time and places where we lived, my parents were extraordinary—although when I was a teenager, I could not clearly see the gift they'd given me. It was only years after I'd earned my PhD that my parents told me they'd had expectations for me. Earlier in my life, they had hoped I would graduate from high school and earn my diploma. That seemed like a worthy goal to them, given the struggles I had with school and my defiance toward teachers and school principals. Astoundingly, even though they had aimed low in their goals, they continued to encourage me in my endeavors, educational and otherwise. At the time, I thought they were

the worst parents ever and was mortified to be seen in public
with them. Now that I am a parent to teenagers, I realize that
this dodge—a technique my boys are just now testing—is not
unusual. And, also, not amusing. Still, young people gain a
necessary kind of distance from their parents as they ask hard
questions about life and faith, and if that distance sometimes
includes ducking down in the passenger seat when driving
through the middle of town, so be it.

I NOW KNOW MY PARENTS' WILLINGNESS to let
their kids ask hard questions about life and pursue their own
faith journeys was somewhat unique, especially for people in
a fairly conservative church tradition like mine. Talking with
other adults has highlighted that uniqueness. I hear many peers
lament that their parents' rigid theological worldview made no
room for questioning or doubt, and that expectations about
faith they developed as children complicate their relationships
now, with parents and faith communities, and with God. Those
who have moved away from the religious ideologies of their
parents still struggle to develop a different identity as believers.
From this complex sifting of religious expectation, at least, my
parents' own openness has spared me.

But my parents were far from perfect, because they are
human, and there were countless other ways that my familial
roots established expectations for me, letting me know that I
was not enough just as I was, and that change was necessary
if I was to be the person God meant me to be. While my mom
was telling me explicitly that I needed to be my own self, she
was also modeling behavior that let me know she never fully
believed *she* was an image-bearer of the divine, nor that she

was worthy of being called a child of God. Mom came by this struggle honestly, having learned from *her* mother the same message that she was not worthy, because of being a woman. Being poor. Being from the wrong side of town. Being born. I have no doubt that my mom wanted to give me freedom to explore life on my terms, that she wanted me to be a strong-willed and opinionated girl, even when doing so meant calls from the principal, the teacher, the Loyal Workers sponsor. Yet she was also giving me contrary messages by her constant self-effacement, which conveyed to me that feeling unworthy was part and parcel of what it meant to be a Christian woman.

Many people feel the expectations of their family of origin more intensely than anything else: more than the popular culture they consume, more than the words they use, more than the stories they tell (though familial expectations can be embedded in stories as well). Perhaps we weight these expectations as somehow more significant because we love and honor the people who shape us and challenge us. Perhaps we give them more credence because we don't want to disappoint those closest to us. When we address the genesis of expectation, then, we also need to question the messages we get from our families, explicitly or not. We need to acknowledge that this messaging is intense, even in families in which the love for each other runs deep and in which parents do their best to allow kids to be exactly who they were created to be.

I didn't know my grandma Mary Schmidt well. She died when I was eight, only months after we moved to Kansas to live closer to her. Well before her death, she had closed up her small house next to Bethel College and moved to a nursing home called Friendly Acres, a name which now seems a misnomer given how poorly my grandma was treated there. Poor treatment had been part of her life story at any rate, starting with the death of her mom when she was quite young and her father's subsequent marriage to a woman who showed far more favor to her own children than to Mary and who berated Mary for being less beautiful, less smart, less gifted than her own offspring.

In this sense, Grandma Schmidt's childhood has a fairy-tale veneer to it, her consistent suffering at the hands of a cruel stepmother reminiscent of a Cinderella story, though without the happy ending. When my grandma married my grandfather, the mockery she endured shifted from her stepfamily to her in-laws, who enjoyed teasing her by using a derogatory Low German word that denoted her unworthiness because she lived on the wrong side of Goessel, Kansas. They criticized my grandma for being too fat, sometimes patting her stomach or backside as a means of ridicule. It's hard to imagine enduring a lifetime of criticism without internalizing and believing everything you've been told about yourself. I imagine my grandma ultimately thought she was unworthy, with no one giving her a different narrative at all.

My grandfather died of advanced colon cancer when my mom was a first-year student in college, leaving my grandma to care for their farm alone until she moved to North Newton. She lived as a poor widow for seventeen years. When she died in 1976, my mom told me her body had given out from exhaustion, something I could only understand as an adult, looking at the sum of my grandma's life and the hardships she endured. Hardships, and heartache. I feel great sadness for the many ways my grandma did not receive love or affirmation in her life. She wore her low self-esteem as a heavy yoke, and even though I didn't know my grandma well, I remember this trait: the ease with which she denigrated herself and the consistent willingness to sacrifice all her comfort or joy for everyone else, even when doing so came with significant costs to her own well-being. Grandma Schmidt knew that she was not good enough, just as she was, and made sure that everyone in her orbit knew this about her too.

One of those people was my mom, who accepted Grandma Schmidt's self-hatred and made it her own. For years, as Mom was raising my two siblings and me, I heard her say that she wasn't very smart. That she didn't have any gifts. That she was a bad cook and a mediocre homemaker. That her work with elementary school students who had disabilities was not that important. That she was too fat and unattractive.

None of this was true, of course, but convincing my mom otherwise was not an option. Indeed, my mom lived by this "truth" of her own insufficiency. She always considered everyone else's needs but her own, sometimes to ridiculous ends, like claiming she *liked* the burnt crusts of bread so the rest of us could eat the more palatable insides. I grew up knowing that Christian women succumbed to this kind of sacrifice because we were not worthy of anything better.

My dad's family conveyed an entirely different set of expectations, sending messages that confused love with food and being happy with being full. Those expectations have complicated my relationship with food and exercise and have led me to believe that being worthy means being thin and physically fit. But I would argue that my mom's familial heritage—and the root of their expectations—has been more persistent for me, perhaps because I learned how to be a woman from the women in my life. Despite my feminist inclinations, I've consistently believed the lie that being a woman means being less than enough.

Most of us can articulate the expectations created by our families of origin. Or I should say *could* articulate, if only we allowed ourselves to think introspectively about our family systems without feeling the guilt that is a frequent companion to our wondering. In a therapy session last year, I finally felt capable of questioning the messages my parents conveyed to me about worthiness. What probably seemed obvious to everyone else had finally occurred to me too. At forty-eight years old, I understood for the first time why the family roots I cherish and love have also limited me from believing that I was a worthy person, just as I am. And I finally understood that I needed to say enough: Enough of the maternal modeling of low esteem. Enough of the inner turmoil, reminding me of my unworthiness as a woman. Enough of a familial cycle.

Enough of feeling I am not enough, just as I am.

Extricating myself from those expectations has been difficult, as I'm sure it is for anyone whose roots are so intertwined with family and church tradition that everything seems like a muddle. Fundamentally, we need to consider the messages we've received from our families and churches and must be willing to call out those negative messages that tell us we are not enough. If we can even begin to ask questions about how our roots have affected us, we will be transformed by the renewing of our minds. We can work to create a world expecting only us, just as we are, rather than someone else entirely.

My mother hosted a family reunion several years ago in Oregon, and her siblings (two brothers and two sisters) came, along with some of my cousins, who were almost strangers to me. I would be hard-pressed to recognize some of my first cousins if they passed me on the street. The fact that we share deep familial roots through our long-dead grandparents amazes me—roots that connect us to a place where none of us live anymore, and to a history that is slowly vanishing.

One evening during that reunion, we sat on the deck into the night, candles flickering on the faces of my aging relatives and their offspring, talking about our families and careers, the roles we play and how they define us. I looked at my aunts, strong women who have persisted through sometimes difficult circumstances. I wondered whether they also carried the trait that defined Grandma Schmidt, the tendency toward self-effacement and a belief that she was not worthy enough, just as she was. And I sat by my cousin, a woman I hadn't seen for almost thirty years, wondering if she also believed herself to be not enough, despite her successful career as a children's writer, including a nomination for the Minnesota Book Award.

Coming together with family on a warm Oregon night, I felt a renewed sense of gratitude for my family's heritage, for the strength my grandma had to persist despite messages telling her she was not worthy. This family that now gathered bore witness to another reality. We were living, loving proof that my grandma's existence mattered, and that her better qualities, including her love for others and her courage, could be traced through her children. Just like our shared Mennonite heritage, the roots of our family run deep and sustain us, which should be—which one day *will* be—enough.

4

THERE'S A PROBLEM WITH YOU GUYS

At least a dozen women were sitting at the table that night, stuck in a corner room of the sports bar, away from the multitude of blaring flat-screen television sets, each showing a baseball game or NASCAR race. I could barely hear my friends asking benign questions about the menu as the whoops of fans riveted to one screen or another broke into our much more sedate contemplation of the relative merits of garlic fries and cheesy pretzels. Most of the women at our table that night were over sixty and had been active in the Christian feminist movement for much of their adult lives. Their cardigan sweaters and proper hairstyles concealed firebrand activist hearts.

Each time the server approached our table, he addressed the collective group as "you guys": "What would you guys like to drink?" "Are you guys ready to order?" The server was congenial, a friendly young adult who probably assumed we were grandmothers and mothers out for a rousing night on the town. He had no idea he was making a rhetorical faux pas until one of the women spoke up.

"You are going to need to stop calling us guys," Jann said, her sweet Texas drawl betraying none of the irritation I know she felt. "We are not guys. We are women, and will be addressed as such."

The server fumbled with his words, trying to apologize—for what, he probably wasn't certain. Surely he'd used "you guys" as a blanket term many times before, and here was someone telling him this phrase was incorrect. For the rest of that evening, though, as baseball games and car races droned on over the bar's din, the server addressed the group more respectfully, doing away with "you guys" altogether.

There was a time when I would have been embarrassed by Jann's insistence that she be called a woman rather than a "guy"—a time when I wouldn't have even heard the dissonance in a phrase a waiter used to address a group of older women. Even though I'd studied English and received a PhD in composition and rhetoric, the significance of the rhetorical choices we make wasn't always on my radar. Back in my twenties, I'd had numerous conversations—scratch that—*arguments* with a roommate about the need for inclusive language. She believed we needed to stop using language driven by patriarchy, that we shouldn't assume *mankind* was synonymous with *humankind*. My roommate even had the audacity to assert that praying to "God the Father" was somehow akin to sexism, as it reinforced the idea that God was a man, whereas God was beyond gender.

"You're being ridiculous," I told her during one especially heated debate. Of course God wasn't a mighty Santa, riding fluffy clouds, white beard and all, even if I still called him my heavenly Father. "Maybe those people who had bad relationships with their fathers will want to choose a different way to understand God," I said. "But *my* relationship with *my* dad is pretty great, and I have no problem whatsoever calling God my father."

Ridiculous indeed.

When I was a few decades older and wiser, I finally figured out what my roommate meant. Sometimes I want to track her down and apologize for the discussions I remember all too clearly: for my rigid insistence that the language I chose didn't have any bearing on my perception of the world, of God, of others; and for my assertion that those who believed God could be just as much a mother as a father had a host of daddy issues they needed to work through. My roommate was merely trying to explain an idea I now understand much more clearly: the language we use matters, a lot, in how we understand the world in which we live.

Language matters so much because our word choices set up expectations for others, compelling us to define people, consciously or not, in ways that may limit their potential as image-bearers of God. Words also convey the sense that some people are more worthy than others. But we don't really want to believe that, so contemporary conversations about the propensity of language to marginalize others are too often discharged with emphatic pronouncements like "That's so politically correct," or "I'm not changing how I talk, because I'm not PC," or "Lighten up! Don't be so easily outraged." These dismissals, often used to justify language that might be blatantly offensive, seek to diminish the significant power that words have in shaping the way we see the world.

Although I want to recognize that our language choices can convey expectations that sometimes serve as barriers to others,

I don't mean to suggest we should avoid difficult ideas, or even words, altogether. Communicating can be tricky, and at times, challenging conversations will cause unintended offense. The tendency to quell potentially risky discussions has been a central critique of the overreach caused by what people term "political correctness." This point has been argued well in "The Coddling of the American Mind," a 2015 *Atlantic* essay that had wide play in academic circles. There, Greg Lukianoff and Jonathan Haidt argue that colleges coddle students with so-called trigger warnings and safe spaces, thus separating young adults from challenging ideas.[1]

I'm not sure what's wrong with having safe spaces, although as a college professor I recognize that difficult conversations about race, gender, sexuality, and power must be part of a liberal arts education. Of a *life* education, really. I've tried to make my classroom a safe space for all students while also hosting these conversations. We need to learn to be careful in our communication, and I've tried in my teaching to avoid conveying expectations to students that would box them in, that would limit their potential. Despite widespread insistence that "being PC" has neutered our cultural conversation, my students would affirm the assertion that language is terribly powerful. The numerous writers we study as part of our curriculum have acknowledged as much over time; their very work validates the idea that what we write and speak shapes our understanding of the world. I also remind students that Jesus, coming to earth as the Word, is emblematic of the power that language has to break through our understanding of the world, transforming everything.

That language shapes our perceptions has not always been a settled fact. Stanford professor Lera Boroditsky has dedicated much of her research to discovering and using empirical tests to prove that language shapes thought. According to Boroditsky, "Language is a uniquely human gift, central to our experience of being human. Appreciating its role in constructing our mental lives brings us one step closer to understanding the very nature of humanity."[2] Although her studies primarily consider how different languages make demands on speakers and listeners, her research with a multitude of languages concludes that the language we use shapes how we understand time and space, colors and objects. Our syntax and diction influence how we experience emotion and our relationships with others and how we make decisions and move through the world. Numerous linguists and neuroscientists have studied the relationship between language and perception, and while they may disagree about *how* that relationship works, most do conclude that language affects what we perceive.

Maybe this is obvious to most people. Yet when I talk in classes (or post on Facebook) about the ways language itself shapes our worldviews, and I suggest that language sometimes conveys unintended expectations for others, I often meet resistance. With accusations that students are being "coddled." With the insistence that the language police have tempered our communication so completely that we can no longer say *anything* without causing offense. In countless conversations about the significance of word choice, I am told that political correctness has run amok and that those who ask for care in how a people group is described are simply being "too PC." From this perspective, calling a group of mature women "you guys" is just friendly banter, and Jann and my crowd were simply meddling in linguistic minutiae.

Think about this, though: Would a waiter ever say to a bar-roomful of mature men, "Hey, gals, what will you be drinking?"

The language we use matters.

Most of us are willing to acknowledge that some words, when used as descriptors for people, are hate-filled, because the words have been used to demean and dehumanize others. I learned this lesson the hard way when, at age five, I used the N-word, testing its power and usefulness with my dad, who taught me swiftly that the word I'd just picked up at recess would not be spoken in our home. When my eldest son was in middle school, he took part in a campaign called "Spread the Word to End the Word," encouraging his peers to stop using the R-word, a derogatory term for people with intellectual disabilities. Kids at his school took a pledge that acknowledged the ways that "language affects attitudes, and attitudes affect actions."[3] Middle school kids can recognize how a word might shape the expectations we have for others. They know that the weight of those negative expectations can affect others, and they are aware of the power we have to shift reality by simply refraining from normalizing words that assert some people are less worthy than others.

So why is talking to others about language choice so incredibly fraught? Some of my most difficult conversations with institutional administrators and religious leaders center on the use of inclusive language. I'm met with defensiveness when I ask others to consider using person-first language—that is, language that describes a person first, followed by that person's identifiers (calling someone a person with physical disabilities, for example, rather than a "disabled person" or a "handicapped person"). Still, I persist in talking about why our words matter because I have a steadfast belief that our language, perhaps more than anything else, establishes how we see

God, and thus how we see each other—expectations we rarely question because they are so deeply entrenched, so central to our culture. Our words have helped to form a world where, more often than not, we are asked to be somebody other than who we were created to be.

ACKNOWLEDGING THAT LANGUAGE MATTERS can produce anxiety, because any change in language about God can actually change the way we view God. If that's the case, we might want to start with the easy work: recognizing that small shifts in language can have huge consequences for the expectations we establish for others, as well as for ourselves.

At least that's been my tack as the advisor for my university's student newspaper. Part of my job includes reading copy before each edition goes to press. I'm not big on censoring students, and have only vetoed one article during my ten-year tenure as advisor: an April Fools' Day piece that involved cannibalism, the cafeteria, and a retirement center in town. (Don't ask.) Even though my student editors are free to write about almost anything they please, they are definitely aware of several words and phrases I loathe. Few things irritate me more than students writing about college-aged women as "girls," as in "the girls' dorms"—especially when *girls* is coupled with college-aged *men*, as in "the girls' dorms and the men's dorms." Nor do I let my writers describe our women's sports teams as "the Lady Bruins" and the men's teams as "the Bruins." These changes probably seem like linguistic fussiness. But, I say to my staff, if we have "Bruins" and "Lady Bruins," we suggest that the women's teams are not fully Bruin, and that women's teams are somehow modified by the norm of the men's teams.

Calling college women "girls" also diminishes them, making them younger than they really are and separating them from the men with whom they are studying. Several years ago at a faculty meeting, one of my colleagues spoke about the handful of "girls" in his class who were not as vocal as the "men" he was also teaching. He wanted to know how he could help the "girls" participate more in a major that was traditionally male-dominated.

Another colleague, sitting behind him, said, "It would probably help if you stopped calling them girls. They are women." I wanted to raise my fist in solidarity, because that one comment had diagnosed a small but significant way we establish expectations with our language alone. By calling students "girls" and "men," my colleague was doing what countless others do: distinguishing the work of male students from that of the dilettantes who are female, still at girls' play even as they are earning degrees.

Some of my students probably roll their eyes when I give my Lady Bruins lecture each year, wondering what the big deal is, why I am so insistent. Perhaps some people think I'm a killjoy, or that there are far more important things to police than our language. What about the world's greatest tragedies, someone might ask? Why critique the inconsequential words we use when children are dying in Aleppo, when terrorist organizations are careening planes into buildings and trucks into crowded markets?

Certainly our attention, our resources, our efforts, and our prayers need to be focused on the world's sorrow, a sorrow compounded by the pain that rains down on the just and the unjust alike. But listen: If we are not willing to consider the ways the words we use shape our perception of the world, and if we are not willing to intentionally change the way we talk about and to each other, how will we ever contend with larger, more evil forces in the world? If we cannot bear to make this small change in our linguistic habits, finding energy to confront large-scale inequity seems significantly more daunting. If we understand that the words we choose can create barriers keeping others from being who God created them to be, shouldn't we be willing to alter our ways of speaking?

It could be that my vocation as an English professor makes me more attuned to language. If I didn't believe that words matter, I probably wouldn't spend countless hours each semester commenting on student essays, suggesting a changed word here or a different sentence structure there, hoping to help others learn how to express ideas more clearly. Because I teach at a Christian university, my responses to students' work sometimes pushes them to describe their faith experiences in ways a broad audience can understand. For some students, the idea that Christian clichés might hold little meaning for readers outside their own religious community is a real discovery. One student told me years after the fact that by asking her to explain more concretely what it meant to "have a walk with the Lord," my hastily written comment on her essay had been transformative. It had helped her consider more carefully how she expressed her life as an evolving person of faith.

Words matter. They really do.

In a Christmas meditation, Quaker writer Parker Palmer focuses on John 1:14: "And the Word became flesh and dwelt among us . . . full of grace and truth" (ESV). Palmer explores the disconnect between the good words we utter—words like *love*, *truth*, and *justice*—and the ways we act in the world. "In personal relations and politics, the mass media, the academy and organized religion," Palmer writes, "our good words tend to float away even as they leave our lips, ascending to an altitude where they neither reflect nor connect with the human condition." The celebration of Jesus' birth each year reminds us that God wrapped love, truth, and justice in human form. The incarnation is a reflection of the Word made flesh to walk among us:

> An infant in a manger is as vulnerable as we get. What an infant needs is not theological debate but nurturing. The same is true of all the good words seeded in our souls that cry out to become embodied in this broken world. If these vulnerable but powerful parts of ourselves are to find the courage to take on flesh—to suffer yet survive and thrive, transforming our lives along with the life of the world—they need the shelter of unconditional love.[4]

Palmer ends his Christmas reflection by inviting us to "allow good words to take flesh" in ourselves, to "incarnate words of life," and to recognize the good words that reside deep in the center of each person on earth.[5]

What an amazing idea: that through our love and care for others we can call forth that of God in each other. Yet doing so requires that we recognize the power of words, both "words of life" and words of death, to create expectations for others. We also have to prepare ourselves for incarnation by asking essential questions—and being willing to hear the answers: Do we use language that calls out life? Or do we use language, sometimes unconsciously, that fails to acknowledge others' humanness, the very ways each individual bears evidence of the divine? Does our language convey our sense that others are worthy, or does it establish expectations that cannot always be met, creating divisions between people? If we are to make space for the Word to live within us, we need to take caution with our words, knowing that even simple changes in the way we say something can entirely transform our relationship to another, and to the Creator as well.

AFTER YEARS OF GRADUATE SCHOOL, of writing and teaching, of learning about the structure and history and significance of language, it was my friend Leslie who taught me most about the power of words. When I first met one of my closest friends four years ago, I remember being rather daunted by how poised she was—how smart, how capable. She was teaching a weightlifting class I'd finally convinced myself to take, certain my weak arms and lack of coordination would make me look a fool among the other fitness freaks at the gym. Leslie put me at ease immediately, and after a few classes, I recognized the intentional work she was doing to make everyone feel welcomed, from those whose weight bars bent under the heavy plates they lifted to folks like me, sweating under the strain of three-pound barbells. As I got to know Leslie through a series of serendipitous events that eventually found us running together most days of the week, I discovered that her longing to create inclusion is one of her many admirable qualities. Central to her advocacy for inclusion is her belief that person-first language can significantly shift our perceptions.

Over the course of our friendship, Leslie has attuned my ears to the problematic nature of language that is not person-first. She has pointed out the many places, including in publications from large institutions, in advertisements, and of course on social media, where those with disabilities are called "disabled people" or "handicapped people," or even "the handicapped." I have seen her gracefully challenge parents to stop defining their children by their diagnoses, as in "my autistic child," or "my Down's kid." My friend has argued, in many different settings, that using these kinds of descriptors defines those with disabilities *by* their disabilities rather than by who they really are. A child with autism has many other defining qualities, as does someone who has a disability. Even when we recognize this—even when we *know* that a person is more than her disability—the language itself shapes how we see someone, how we interact with her, what we expect that person can offer us and the world. For example, if we see a man primarily for his physical disability, we may decide he deserves our pity and our prayers for healing, rather than acknowledging that his disability is but one part of his story; that our understanding of what healing looks like might not be his understanding; and that he might love who he is and who God has created him to be.

Although person-first language is fundamental to disability rights advocacy, the same principle can, and should, be applied to all people, at all times. This is something else my friendship with Leslie has taught me: that any true sense of community, of inclusion, requires that we see people first, rather than their identifiers. In some ways, this principle has been organic for me, because I recognize the ways my language will shape how others perceive my family or me. I never introduce my kids as "my adopted sons," but only as "my sons," acknowledging that the descriptor *adopted* might set up expectations for what our relationship should be. (Besides, most mothers do not introduce their offspring as "my biological sons.") In other ways, learning to use person-first language has presented more of a challenge, and I've had to remind myself to consider people first. This is true when I talk about my own parents, who are not "old people" but whose age is only one of their many identities; and when I discuss those who identify as LGBT, who are not "gay men" or "lesbian women" or (more egregiously) "homosexuals," but people for whom, as with all of us, sexual identity is only one part of their far more complex, far richer, selves.

Perhaps the idea of using person-first language is not so novel. Yet those who insist on person-first language, like my friend Leslie, face significant resistance from those who cannot believe that word choice really matters. I see this resistance play out time and time again: when Leslie suggests that someone change the way his Facebook post describes another person and she gets a defensive response in reply; when she talks face-to-face with a mother who insists on calling her son a "special needs kid who rides the short bus." Some might quibble that "special needs" is an appropriate term, not derogatory in the least, although even defining someone as "special" sets him apart from his peers, his needs distinctive and cloyingly precious in ways they are not for others. Introducing one's own child to strangers as "special" and a rider of the "short bus" will, whether a mom realizes it or not, set up expectations for her child—expectations that will stand in the way of that child being perceived as the whole, and holy, person God has created him to be.

In my writing classes, I talk about the connection between the universal and the individual so often and so passionately that I imagine my students might just mimic me behind closed doors—right down to the ways I hold up my arms and shut my eyes, as if I'm in a contemporary Christian worship band. Perhaps I do this because I believe so ardently that our personhood is holy and to be honored and that we are each fearfully, uniquely, and wonderfully made. This is fundamentally what person-first language gives us: an opportunity to honor both the universal and the individual, as well as the chance to defy the expectations foisted on us by a label.

In the aftermath of the 2016 presidential election, the poet Jeanne Murray Walker reflected on the diminishing power of words that convey truth. "In a country where words are no longer hinged to truthful meaning, one word becomes just like another," she writes. And yet Walker refuses to relinquish the ability of words to change the world, to link one person to another, to give us empathy and insight, if only we are bold enough to speak, or write, truthfully. "Words," she says, "are only scraps of sound, rags of wind, bits of vibration we shape like music with our tongues and teeth and breath. But if you're reading this, words are where the two of us are meeting. Words help us grasp one another, they nerve us to go on."[6] Making one small linguistic shift allows us to see and know people differently, to find connection through our shared humanity, no matter who we are.

AND SO I WONDER: Can we also change the language we use to think and talk about God? In the last few years especially, my ears have become acutely attuned to the ways people address God. I imagine colluding with Christian feminists will have that effect on almost anybody. For much of church history, language about God has focused on God's masculine qualities, so much so that we rarely considered the feminine metaphors used in the Bible to define God's character. But such metaphors exist, in spades, and a close reading of the Bible reveals that God is not only a lord and king and almighty judge but also a hen, a mother bear, a woman in labor, moaning as she gives birth to a new people. The birthing metaphor is central to the Gospels, to Nicodemus being born again. In this instance, God as mother brings forth a spiritual rebirth; the language of born-again Christian remains an important part of the contemporary Christian lexicon.

When Christians talk about God, the language we use rarely acknowledges the diverse characteristics of God, instead focusing more on God's masculine traits: on the power and might and strength and judgment God offers God's people. Although using primarily masculine language (and in many cases, solely masculine language) to address God is deeply embedded in many Christian communities, failing to address a more multifaceted God also creates division, codifying a perception of God that marginalizes others and limits them from believing that they too bear the image of their Creator. Of all the conversations I have about the power of language as it relates to perception, conversations in which I suggest that people use inclusive terms for God have been the most difficult. But even so, these conversations are also necessary in making space for others to be who God created them to be.

Many Christians affirm that God is neither male nor female, and that because God exists outside our human comprehension, God also exists outside our human understanding of gender. I have had countless discussions with fellow believers who acknowledge that God does not have a prescribed gender but who still contend that using masculine language for God is right, necessary, even biblical.

The foundation of such arguments seems to be this: God is not male or female, *but* . . .

because the Bible calls God he, and Father, and Lord, and King, all masculine words;

and because Jesus, on the cross, calls out to his Father, and throughout the Gospels recognizes God as Father;

and because the Christian story necessitates a trinity of Father, Son, and Holy Ghost;

and because our church fathers and church traditions and church hymns use masculine language to address God,

we must also do the same. Even when doing the same means missing out on the opportunity to understand and worship God differently. Even when doing so might mean conveying to some people groups that they are considerably less worthy than others.

What if, when we talked about God, we were able to acknowledge that God is infinitely more than our language can describe? What if we could try on some of the less-used metaphors for God that exist in the Bible, testing how those other metaphors might change the way we know God and also each other? What if we could recognize that the way we talk about God is deeply embedded in our cultures, that it shapes our perceptions of each other, and that it defines who we consider worthy of love and acceptance?

In *A Gentler God*, author Doug Frank explores the idea that our understanding of God is shaped by twentieth-century Christian culture. Frank writes that the metaphors we now use for God are not based on inviolate truths but rather reflect culture. *A Gentler God* provides a historical context for the images of God that have predominated in modern Christianity, especially those that portray God as vindictive and angry, a petulant judge willing to exact a blood sacrifice from his own Son as payment for how evil humanity has become. But the character of Jesus, and the entire story of the Gospels, provides a far different image of God, one founded not on God's desire to judge and condemn us but on a God whose essence is love and who wants to be in relationship with us.[7] Frank uses the life and ministry of Jesus in the Gospels as his guide, convincingly arguing that Jesus was crucified not to bear God's punishment but to share in our own human brokenness. *A Gentler God* also shows what might happen when we believe this biblical narrative instead of embracing the drumbeat of evangelicalism's defining story and its grumpy Father.

Reading Frank's book, I realized how the language we've used to describe God also reflects our understanding of God and of each other. If we embrace language that sees God as a gracious, loving Creator rather than an almighty Judge, we will begin to recognize as well that it is not only the strong and the powerful who reflect aspects of the Creator. Because our language so assuredly shapes our reality, voicing that God is more than a King and a Lord (or even an angry Father) influences our ability to understand that we all reflect aspects of the Creator.

I am grateful that the work of early Christian feminists clearly—and courageously—claims this truth: until a different kind of God language is used in our churches and religious institutions, in our songs and in our prayers, equity for all will be impossible. Christian feminist mothers like Letha Dawson Scanzoni and Virginia Ramey Mollenkott have spent their lifetimes pointing to this reality. And yet, as Mollenkott said recently, most churches, both mainline and evangelical, continue to use male-centered language to talk about God. In a 2017 address, Mollenkott described a time when, after speaking to a congregation about honoring the feminine biblical imagery for God, she was approached by a woman who wondered if Mollenkott had "forgotten that God was holy." The incident, Mollenkott said, reflected the sense that so long as we believe God is white, and male, we will likewise believe that only those who are white and male are considered sacred. This belief alone justifies injustice done to those who don't reflect this image of God. Using more expansive language calls attention to the sacredness of all people, she said, and is necessary if we are to create space for all people to become who God means them to be.[8]

Those who persist in referring to God through exclusively masculine metaphors perpetuate a church in which masculine traits are sacrosanct. Consequently, both men and women must fight rigid expectations that often don't fit them well. When God is male, those who identify as male become godlike.[9] In the book's next section, I will explore more about what this has meant in terms of expectations for men and women, and how the continuation of a patriarchal culture, endorsed by an understanding of a masculine God, has often made it nearly impossible for women to live fully into their callings. This weight of expectation can be overwhelming, especially when it's also freighted with the sense that God has ordained people to fulfill specific roles—and that roles held by the powerful are somehow more holy, more worthy, than any others.

Creator-first language changes all of that: it prioritizes God's essential characteristic as the Creator—as someone who formed us and called us good. Recognizing that we are, all of us, created in God's image allows us to celebrate the vast beauty of God's remarkably diverse creation in which each of us singularly reflects aspects of the divine. If we can acknowledge that we are all created in God's image—that we share the same source, the same Parent, the same intimacy with the Creator—we likewise acknowledge the interplay of the individual and the universal writ large. We each wholly reflect the image of the divine while also being fearfully, wonderfully, and uniquely ourselves.

Changing our language makes this acknowledgment possible, and in a world where even the words that we use construct expectations for who we are to be, paying careful attention to those words can have significant consequences for how we see ourselves, others, and God.

Part II

FINDING YOURSELF

5

SEARCHING FOR THE GOOD LIFE

It took three trips down the aisle as a bridesmaid for me to decide this wedding business was really a crock. Halfway to the altar in a very big church with a very big center aisle, I wanted to bust out laughing. Here I was, in teal off-the-shoulder taffeta, tottering slowly, step by step, in high-heeled shoes dyed the same color as my dress. Here I was, wearing the dress I'd paid for, as well as the shoes I'd paid for, both having put a significant dent in my graduate school stipend. Here I was, taking mincing steps to the front, the shoes already cutting into my toes and making me feel even more ridiculous. Several other useless dresses were stuffed into my bedroom closet at home, dresses the same color as several other heels I'd worn only one day and then abandoned. At age twenty-five, I found that being a bridesmaid and never the bride had finally chipped away any remaining semblance of my self-esteem. There, in the middle of that church aisle, I wanted to throw my teal bouquet at the beaming bride and bolt, perhaps giving a middle finger to the congregation before storming out for good.

I had a little bit of an anger problem back then, especially when it came to weddings. Or maybe I should say wedding culture, from which I felt entirely excluded for most of my twenties. As a single person, I was expected to soon settle down with my beloved, start a family, and get started on the American dream. But as a victim of the Christian college "ring by spring" mythology, I graduated without having found The One and was left wondering what was wrong with me. Why had every single one of my friends found a mate, experienced the most clever proposal ever, and begun planning a wedding, all while I was still waiting for my first kiss? The language that people used at the time only exacerbated my sense that God was punishing me by keeping me single. My friends talked about being "blessed," about God giving them "the greatest gift *ever*." By implication, those who hadn't landed The One in college were not blessed, were not worthy of God's great gift of a spouse.

Through my early twenties, I tried to remain hopeful, certain the man of my dreams was waiting right around life's next corner. I saw a potential blessing everywhere—in the church pews, in my graduate school classes, in line at the nearby bakery—and stopped seeing men as anything but potential candidates for God's greatest gift.

When both my siblings got married in the same month and I was still very much single at twenty-six, I began to despair, my slowly simmering anger rolling into a full boil. I couldn't sit in church anymore, not when every young adult around me seemed to be paired off or already starting families. Not when church activities always focused on families, siloing singles into the hapless corner of any gathering. Not when sermons reminded me that marriage and family were God's greatest blessings—blessings I was increasingly sure would never find me.

There were good things happening in my life during my twenties. I spent a year doing social work in Pittsburgh, and my world expanded as I spent days in the high-rise projects of the city's East End. I went to graduate school, got a master's degree in Missouri and then a doctorate in Oklahoma. During the summers, I accepted manual labor jobs I hated but that taught me a lot about hard work in midwestern humidity and about how to plant flowers and spread mulch. I bunked with my grandma in small-town Illinois for a while, and I saw what she loved about the community she'd settled in for more than sixty years. I lived in several dumpy apartments and spent nights in the library studying for comprehensive exams, which I passed with distinction.

But because I wasn't married, and because I hadn't found the solid career or upward mobility that a new college graduate is promised, I spent my twenties also feeling incomplete. My life lacked the traction that I had assumed was part of being a college graduate. Because I wasn't wedded to The One, people didn't always know what to do with me—not even my own parents, who asked often whether I'd started dating yet and who breathed a huge sigh of relief when, at age twenty-nine, I finally received a marriage proposal.

Western culture, and especially Christian culture, has a clear narrative for what our lives are supposed to look like, the course they are supposed to take. That narrative includes the belief—sometimes sublimated, but often not—that we will become settled as young adults, find spouses, have kids, enjoy family and career, spoil grandkids, and enter retirement satisfied with a life's work well done. These are presented to us as incontrovertible truths, as if we are all guaranteed the same trajectory. We are promised that our lives will be as rigid (but wonderful!) as the Life board game, the road we travel mapped out in vivid colors, with clearly defined stops for our education, a spouse, and 2.5 kids. The only uncertainty is whether those kids will be pink or blue.

What happens, though, when we find ourselves heading in a different direction than the one we've been promised? When the cards we draw don't offer us a clear path? What happens when we internalize the myth that our lives have to take a certain form to be worthy? What happens when we believe that the journey we're on is not acceptable, just as it is?

My life has gone off-script enough for me to know what happens, at least to some degree. People in your family will ask, "Why aren't you married yet?" when you are twenty-eight and single, and you will spend a lot of time squeezed into events as the third wheel, because the world is essentially built for pairs. People will also wonder, secretly, "What's *wrong* with her?" This applies to those who remain single too long, who are childless, or who experience complications like a mental health diagnosis or a difficult birth or infidelity in marriage. In such instances, we are inclined to believe that life hasn't been predictable for a reason, and we seek ways to blame those who wander away from the life map we've been given.

But the truth is that the script itself is problematic. Rather than celebrating the diversity of life experiences that God gives us, we tend toward sameness. Like my teal-dyed shoes and my ridiculous bridesmaid role, we fold ourselves into expectations for how our lives will look. Those expectations often make us angry and depressed, make us certain we have somehow failed or that God has not delivered what was promised. For Christians, the script even suggests that the life pathway we follow is the one blessed by God, and those who choose a different way are outside of God's favor. Those who are forced onto another road because of life's circumstances are often considered "tragic" or unredeemable; in some cases, rather than helping people navigate these difficult times, we believe something is wrong with them, even that God is punishing them for some unforgivable sin or for lacking faith.

If only I could have resisted the narrative that said I had to wear teal shoes to be a good friend. If only I could have said no to the same narrative that told me I had to march down a long aisle in a wedding dress to truly be happy and that I needed a spouse to be blessed. If only we could do this for one another, tearing up the script and allowing each other to pursue our own unique paths or accept with more peace a life journey we could not have anticipated walking. But too often we just feel miserable, or ridiculous, or angry enough to flip off a congregation that just wants, for goodness sake, to see a wedding.

IT OFTEN TAKES BEING SINGLE to recognize how much of our culture is skewed toward couples. I'm not talking about young adult singlehood but about the kind that can stretch on for years, sharpening your perspective about how lonely the single life can be when the world is built for two. Every action of others seems intended to highlight your single status, and those who are happily coupled cannot seem to remember what it feels like to be alone. The singlehood slights can seem insignificant, but people who are single know how even small acts can amplify a sense of unworthiness.

Our culture, including our church culture, has an uncomfortable relationship with singleness. In multiple ways, we are encouraged to embrace being single and independent; but then we are also told that our deepest fulfillment will come from partnership with another. We hear that "a party of one" is totally acceptable, something to be celebrated, even; but then we see all around us that a party of two is preferable. We imagine that every person walking solo through life feels incomplete without a partner, and our expectation is that being single means being sad and lonely, a creature to be pitied rather than admired.

Think about the images of singleness we see in popular culture, where those who are single seem to fall into two camps. Either they are awkward introverts (schoolmarms or video game junkies living in parents' basements) or they are desperately seeking a partner, their entire reason for being a quest to find someone who completes them. Both depictions are unsettling, because the people in both depictions are unsettled. The former would love another way of life—save that debilitating shyness or inertia which keeps them pinned to their routine. The latter would love another way of life, too, and will pursue it by any means possible, including trying on any number of relationships until The One finally emerges.

Now more than ever, adults in the United States are more likely to be single than married. A 2014 report by the Bureau of Labor Statistics concluded that just over 50 percent of adults in the United States were unmarried; in Canada's most recent census, 28 percent of homes were headed by people who were single.[1] Yet the messages remain: those without a partner are to be pitied, including those who have made an intentional decision to go through life solo. According to a 2014 Huffington

Post article, we are surrounded by messages telling us that singleness leads to loneliness, low self-esteem, and a sense of worthlessness. The article's headline reads "If You Feel Bad about Being Single, It's Not Because You're Single." Instead, it's likely because you have been bombarded by images reminding you that if you're single, you should try to remedy the situation as soon as possible, because the single life is a sad life. Yet surveys show that even though women experience a bump in life satisfaction after marriage, over time, single and married women report similar levels of happiness. Marriage will not necessarily a happier life make.

But those messages about the significant joy that accompanies marriage persist. On most television shows and in most movies, women who appear on screen as independent and strong still pursue romance to the detriment of their professional careers, signaling that finding a partner is what's expected, even for those who want to prioritize work and career. Freelance journalist Ann Friedman says culture has conditioned us to be condescending to single women no matter how successful they might be in other parts of their lives, because we assume that *of course* a single woman wants to be married.[2] This stigma of singleness is more intense for women than for men, clear even in the language we use to describe singleness. A single woman is still sometimes referred to as a "spinster" or an "old maid." A man is simply a bachelor, no matter his age.

These negative representations, and the pressure to marry they represent, fail to account for the many reasons a single life might be preferable to a married one. Some of these reasons come with scientific support: single people are generally healthier and exercise more than their married peers; they report being more self-sufficient and resilient; they have more interests and a wider circle of friends.[3] Lacking any kind of intense self-focus on keeping the family alive and thriving, those who are single often cultivate rich, deep communities, their attention to others reflecting a ministry of hospitality many married people are incapable of extending. The apostle Paul is onto something when he says in 1 Corinthians 7 that it is better to marry than to burn, but better by far to be single.

But despite knowing all of this, the pressure remains high to be happily wedded, especially in Christian circles, where Paul's words on singleness seem to always come with an asterisk, one that essentially says "Being single may be special, but marriage is definitely more biblical, more closely aligned with what God wants for us." There is an entire Christian cultural apparatus set up for adults who are single, with websites, books, blogs, podcasts, dating apps, and church groups intended to help the single folks recognize their "special" place in the world—while also providing mechanisms to get them hitched as quickly as possible. Christians who are single past what seems an appropriate marrying age are met with a slew of clichés reminding them of their state, with Pinterest boards providing canned wisdom about waiting for Prince Charming, for Mrs. Right, for Boaz (who is the prototypical Christian man, apparently, even if he was an Israelite).

"Waiting for Boaz" has actually become the goal of women who are still single and still looking, and social media sites offer singles the opportunity to fantasize about who Boaz might be and what he might be wearing. Women are told they should "dance with God and he will let the perfect man cut in," as if life is some metaphysical high school prom and God a kind placeholder until a dreamy man shows up. It's not clear whether God—or The One—will be paying for the prom tickets. Christian dating advice for singles is informed by the belief that men are designed to pursue their princesses. Women are reminded that the godly thing to do is to wait, pray, and hope someone will ask them out; to do otherwise would show a kind of boldness not becoming of a Christian woman. This way of thinking robs women of their agency.

What the apostle Paul says about being married and burning is a significant piece of the equation for single women and men. Part of the message for single Christians is that sexual abstinence is their special achievement, not a burden to bear but a state to celebrate. Countless websites, magazines, and books for Christian singles focus on the importance of remaining sexually pure until marriage, providing advice for ways to combat sexual desire and the temptations of the flesh. Although 80 percent of evangelical adults admit to having sex before marriage, Christian culture expects singles to remain celibate.[4]

Even before the Christian singleness industry had found full expression on the Internet and through social media, the messages about singlehood existed, serving as a vibrant, ever-present soundtrack to my twenties. I had absorbed the messages about single life completely and knew my life would not be sanctified and blessed until I found a man—or until God found me worthy enough to finally grant me a spouse. My disappointment and sadness followed me through several moves, several failed relationships, several attempts to make a man fit into a suit only my desire to marry had made. My twenties would have been a lot more fun, and a lot less stressful, if I could have pushed back against the multitude of messages I heard about marriage and about finding True Love. When I talk to students—many of whom still seriously despair if they haven't landed a ring by spring—I share my story. I want them to enjoy being young and single and free. I want them to dance and not worry whether the right person will cut in. I want them to find themselves in a different world that tells them they are worthy, single or not.

MY HUSBAND, RON, AND I GOT MARRIED in a small gathering at Tilikum, a Quaker church camp near Newberg. His idea of a perfect wedding included casual attire, a potluck, and a softball game. But his daughter, then seventeen, convinced him that I might not want to get married in jean shorts after the fifth inning. So we compromised, and in September 1997, with my father officiating, we were married in front of a handful of family and friends, with Ron's children serving as witnesses. We paddled away in a canoe afterward to begin a short honeymoon at the Oregon coast. After a weekend's respite, both of us were back at our teaching jobs. Nothing, and everything, had changed.

When I talk about my wedding, people often ask whether I really wanted such a simple affair. My answer is an ambiguous "I don't know." Our wedding didn't put us into debt, unlike most ceremonies these days, where the average cost of a wedding is $35,000. [5] The cheapskate in me would never spend that much for a one-day event, and the total cost of our wedding was closer to $400, much of which was spent on a very nice dress Ron bought for me. After marching down church aisles for plenty of friends' weddings, I couldn't imagine marching down an aisle by myself, nor could I fathom doing something so patriarchal as having my dad give me away to a man at the altar. Furthermore, when Ron and I married I was new to the area, and I do wish more of my friends could have attended my wedding, but I also know that friendships shift and change, and the folks who I would have invited then are not necessarily the ones I might invite now.

Still, despite having fond memories about the day I married Ron, I sometimes wonder if I missed a once-in-a-lifetime opportunity to be a traditional blushing bride. This sense of "what if?" is intensified any time I watch a wedding reality show (of which there are many) or attend a student's marriage ceremony; I am still not immune to the messages I receive in our culture about weddings, even twenty years after my own ceremony. Those messages are powerful and persistent, letting us know that our wedding day will be the best day of our lives and that it needs to be memorable—not only for the bride and groom, but for everyone who attends. No cost should be spared to ensure that guests will be wowed by what they see, and the reception should be a party like no other. We who are Christians learn that abstaining from sex before marriage is essential . . . but on the honeymoon's first night, sex will be mind-blowing, and will remain so forever after. We also are reminded incessantly that marital life is amazing, something to which we should all aspire, even though divorce rates remain relatively high in our country, even for Christians, and even though some fight so ardently to keep marriage rights limited that entire Christian denominations are crumbling. Messages about marriage are mixed enough to make heads spin.

Historically, marriages in the West were far more about family alliances and economic gain than about love; this is still true for some cultures today. In the West, marriages based on love alone have only been prominent since the last century, when the wedded life became an ideal to which normal people were taught to aspire. And I do mean "normal": those who express no desire to marry or who believe arranged marriages are appropriate are seen as aberrant.

Before marriage comes the wedding, though, and this is where most young people seem to invest their energy. The expectation in Western culture is that folks will do up their ceremonies in a big way, to the point that weddings seem almost like competitions—but with nearly everyone using the same rustic materials, the same kind of burlap, the same size of mason jars. Weddings become another place where conformity is desired, with Pinterest and other social media sites providing salient advice. These days, couples are choosing to hold their ceremonies in barns with vintage accents, the clever edginess of these choices tempered only a little because everyone else is doing just about the same thing. If I'd waited long enough, I imagine "cheap wedding by a church camp pond" would have come into vogue too!

AFTER HEARING FOR SO LONG that getting married was the goal to which I could aspire, after believing that my spouse would be The One to complete me, I was surprised by the reality. Marriage is hard work, and that labor began for us about one week after our honeymoon, when I wanted to do chores together and Ron wanted to play video games with his son, who was spending the weekend with us per a custody agreement. This tension about household duties, when they are completed, and whether work comes before play has been a consistent theme in our marriage, without any easy resolution.

Even admitting that we continue to argue about the laundry and the dishwasher and mowing the lawn is difficult, because the expectation is that two adults married for this long should have stuff figured out. Images in popular culture tell us that such arguments are a worthy plotline for a sitcom like *Modern Family*, where Phil Dunphy's inability to complete a simple household job is met with a laugh track. In real life, frustrations are not so funny, especially when I just want someone else to fold the laundry already. I also dislike the other prominent tropes about marriage in popular culture—infidelity, domestic abuse, constant yelling and conflict. Together, these messages suggest that marriages will run either hot or cold, with little in between, including the day-to-day thrum of discord in which many of us live.

For most conservative Christians, too, expectations about marriage are wrapped together with expectations about gender roles, which often complicate relationships unnecessarily. When you are told that your husband should be the head of the household, should make all the decisions, should be your spiritual and personal leader, an untenable power dynamic can result. Women in complementarian marriages—in which it is assumed that gender roles are separate and complement each other—can chafe under expectations that rob them of their agency.

Women often consider themselves fully responsible for conflicts that do arise, then, because they are not submitting themselves fully to their husbands. This notion arises from certain advice on Christian marriage, including that found in Mark Driscoll and Grace Driscoll's *Real Marriage*, which maintains that women need to keep up appearances, else their spouses stray.[6] In similar vein, Pat Robertson, patriarch of the *700 Club*, blamed a woman's looks for her spouse's desertion, saying the woman might not be as sweet as she looks and might, in fact, be "hard-nosed"—all good reasons for a husband to find sustenance elsewhere.[7]

Say what? Marriage is God's greatest gift, but if that gift goes sour, it's because women aren't working hard enough? The Driscolls and Robertson may seem like minority voices on this. Their muscular Christianity—that is, one driven by masculine strength and power—shapes their ideology that women are primarily responsible to keep the home fires burning. But countless other conservative Christians have been saying similar things during the last few decades. The Driscolls and Robertson and others believe ardently in what they call "biblical marriage," the term itself setting up rigid expectations for how our lives should unfold. Although in much of the Bible marriage looked far different than it does today, "biblical marriage" has often been construed as a sacred bond between one man and one woman, one wherein the wife is bound to submit to her husband, who in turn is supposed to love her as Christ loves the church. In practice, "biblical marriage" is often used to include only those who fall inside the bounds of what Christian culture has considered acceptable.

So we consistently hear contradictory messages about love and marriage, and these messages make an unalloyed view of the institution very difficult. Our contemporary conversations about marriage reflect the confused expectations we hold about the married life. We are told that singleness is a special role, for special people . . . but we then spend little time in our churches making sure that singles are seen as whole and holy. Christians affirm that marriage is a partnership entered equally by two consenting adults . . . but then promote a power dynamic that strips women of agency. We are told that marriage is a sacred institution, the bedrock of our communities . . . but then withhold it from LGBT people in committed relationships.

Such expectations, according to the dominant narrative in Christian culture, are fairly clear, but what people often hear is this: You are not worthy of God's love, God's blessing, God's favor, unless you conform. You are not enough.

MAYBE BECAUSE I WAS RELATIVELY OLDER when we married, or because my husband already had kids, or because I was dense and not paying attention, I didn't field many questions about whether Ron and I were going to start a family. I know this is rare, and that couples are often interrogated about their family planning choices, sometimes even before they've been married. But even though nobody asked us, that didn't mean we weren't thinking hard about the choices we needed to make, and for the first five years of our marriage, we went back and forth about what adding several more kids to Ron's two would look like for us. A week after 9/11, in what might seem the most clichéd of decisions, we concluded that there's no time like the present, and that we wanted to make the world a better place, and that love was all we needed to successfully adopt and raise children from a disenfranchised area of the world.

We were so, so naïve.

Over the next few years, we signed with an adoption agency, completed home studies, got on international adoption waiting lists, and eventually brought home two boys: Benjamin Quan, a seven-month-old infant from Vietnam, in 2002; and Samuel Saurabh, a three-year-old toddler from India, in 2005.

During their adoptions, I read a lot about adoption loss, birth family reunification, the corruption that sometimes taints international adoption, and potential risks with attachment and disabilities that are a regular part of adoption, whatever a child's age and whatever the health records might say. When our youngest son's adoption took almost two years, thanks to some irregularities with our adoption agency and an orphanage in Mumbai, what I'd been reading became reality for us, and I wondered often about the baby I'd claimed as mine, half a world away, growing up in India and unaware of the ways his life would one day change irrevocably.

Almost fifteen years after we brought Benjamin home from Vietnam, I cannot imagine having made a different choice for our family. Being a parent was the best choice Ron and I made beyond choosing each other, and I am grateful to be a mother to these two remarkable young men. Even when I'm furious with them for deciding at ten at night that they need supplies for a school project due the next day, or when I'm shivering on ice-cold bleachers, watching my kid play soccer, or on those rare evenings when I agree to watch an episode of *The Simpsons* for the umpteenth time—even on those days I still feel a rush of gratitude that we decided to have children, and that we decided to adopt.

Sometimes, given my great sense of joy, I am tempted to feel an equally great sorrow for those who made a different choice and who decided not to have children. I try to stop myself when my heart and mind indulge that impulse, because I know I am only capitulating to those cultural mythologies that say every person longs to be a parent and that those who decide to live childfree are hapless and pitiable. I need to remind myself that these are projections, and that people who make the intentional choice to remain childfree are not incomplete.

In this as in other things, gender affects the kind of messages received about parenthood. While men may feel some pressure to become dads, those who choose to remain childfree do not endure the same level of scrutiny that women do. Both popular and Christian culture convey countless messages telling them that motherhood is the highest, most honorable calling a woman can have. Critiques of contemporary feminism suggest that the value of motherhood has been undermined in our culture, and that women have become child-hating harpies, the role of mothering one to be reviled. Yet this critique does not have much purchase, and images in popular culture reinforce the idea that being a mother is a most honorable vocation to which every woman should aspire.

Consider, for example, the many "baby bump" stories that appear on entertainment news sites as fans track the reproductive decisions of their favorite stars, celebrating headlines announcing the birth of another child in Hollywood. When an actress passes her prime fertility years without a pregnancy, the same news sites express despair and sadness, and coverage of extraordinarily successful actresses like Jennifer Aniston, lacking the baby who would complete them, becomes increasingly woeful. Advertisements primarily show women as mothers; according to one analysis, when women appear in marketing materials, they are portrayed as mothers over 60 percent of the time.[8]

For Christian women, expectations about motherhood are even more intense, and those who choose to remain childfree face even more scrutiny. Women in the church are told that motherhood is the highest calling for women, the role to which we should, above all else, aspire. The first time a girl is given a baby doll to play with, she begins the grooming necessary for her role as mother. Christian culture puts this grooming on steroids, turning imaginary play into an opportunity for girls to begin developing the skills they will need as mothers. Those who don't feel specifically called to motherhood learn that they will need to continue discerning, and that at some point, their hearts will become open to the role to which God is obviously calling them.

The Gospel Coalition, a prominent voice for evangelicals, articulates well the sentiments of those who believe women are expected to take on motherhood as part their primary vocation, suggesting those Christian women who choose to remain childfree are narcissists, and that in making the choice to forego having children, they also forego thinking about God. Writing for the coalition's website, Kathleen Nielson says choosing to remain childfree means people are not seeing clearly that children are a beautiful gift from God, that rejecting babies means rejecting that gift of life, and that having children is one way to pass salvation on to the next generation.[9] For many Christians, Paul's exhortation in 1 Timothy 2:15 is to be understood literally: "Yet she [woman] will be saved through childbearing . . . if they continue in faith, love, and holiness, with self-control." (NRSV, NKJV). Those women who choose not to give birth are refusing this very important pathway to their own salvation.

And those who cannot conceive? Messages about the godly role of mothering and about motherhood's highest calling affect those women too, often in devastating ways. When it is asserted that women are to be honored for their birth-giving gift, and that God blesses women who bear children, those who struggle with infertility hear a concurrent theme: that infertility is somehow their fault, that God has chosen not to bless them, that they are defective. Even though Ron and I decided not to conceive biologically, I still feel the sting of these messages: that because I did not bear my children, I am not a "real" mother, and that because I haven't experienced pregnancy and childbirth, I have not groaned through the pains of real motherhood. I can only imagine how much worse those who long to be pregnant must feel, hearing that they are defective, spiritually or physically, and that they are being denied God's greatest gift and a mother's highest calling because of their own deficiency. For whatever reason, they are not enough.

Because motherhood is apparently the highest calling for women, expectations are astronomical, especially now, when Pinterest, Facebook, and a zillion blogs let mothers know what they should be doing to make their kids healthy and happy, smart and successful. Both popular and Christian culture excel at dispensing advice targeted at mothers and their longing to be fabulous and to create the Best Kids Ever. We hear that being a good mom means being self-sacrificial in every way, such that all too often, a mom's needs are sublimated completely. In many Christian resources, including blogs and websites, this selflessness is equated to that of Jesus. This essentially elevates a mother to the status of a savior, giving up her life so her children might thrive. We are expected to be messiahs, but without the resources to heal the flu or to make water into wine.

Our children, we are told, are a direct reflection of our parental skills and know-how. Kids who act out or struggle in school are, more often than not, victims of bad parenting, unluckily born to mothers and fathers who cannot rise to societal expectations for what it means to raise good kids. Even before babies come into our homes, we are told how we might increase their IQs and their chances of getting into Ivy League schools. An entire market of toys has been created to help supplement learning at every stage of a child's life so that toddlers learn their numbers and letters and kindergartners learn to read. If I see one more social media post with an image of children quietly enjoying their big stacks of library books and comments from parents congratulating themselves on creating a wonderful culture of literacy, I will probably drop-kick my computer. I do still have that anger problem, but I also chafe against the underlying assumption of such posts: that kids who hate reading have parents who do not prize literacy quite as much. This is often not the case, and sometimes parents can be passionate about reading (and might even teach English at a university) but their children will still see reading as a chore to be endured, and endured with obstinacy, anger, and tears.

Parents are often criticized for reliving their pasts through their children, of pushing their children to succeed so that they too can bask in the heady glory of achievement. I feel this tension regularly: wanting my kids to discover their own interests and gifts apart from my own, but also wondering if their lack of enthusiasm about reading (for example) somehow reflects poorly on me. In the same way, I tend to accept that my younger son's athletic skills reflect well on my parenting and my own athletic ability. The truth is that kids are who they are apart from what we do as parents, both in their successes and in their challenges. My husband has learned this lesson well, having raised one set of children twenty years after raising another. He has found that the parenting approaches he used for his older set proved far less successful with the younger.

It's tempting to believe that our kids will always manifest our great skill as parents, and too often we seem to accept that those children we deem "good" have been raised by parents with the chops to do the job well. We even compliment each other for raising "good kids," unaware that the statement itself implies that those who are struggling must be at fault. Sometimes this is the case, and some adults do lack parenting skills. Often, though, we expect that kids are a direct reflection of their parents' good work—or shoddy work—when in fact there are many factors influencing their behavior.

Heaven help parents of children with significant mental health diagnoses. Or who have disabilities. Or who simply dislike school and traditional learning. For they shall be judged—or their children called "special," which is its own kind of judgment. They shall be marginalized, their children scorned. They will be deemed not good enough as parents, despite their exhausting efforts, because those efforts—and their children—are not what we have certified good, or Christian, or worthy.

HAVING KIDS has sometimes made going to work difficult, especially on those mornings where I've yelled like a banshee for my boys to brush their teeth and then, twenty minutes later, walked into a classroom completely composed, ready to tackle the remarkable world of research writing and MLA citations. Still, I must admit that my job as an English professor is a cakewalk. Really. I know I'm not supposed to say as much—I'm not supposed to lift the veil and let everyone see how relatively easy my vocation is—but let's not kid ourselves here. Being employed as a college professor, especially one with tenure, affords me a flexible schedule, a long summer, and the opportunity to spend my days reading good literature, working on writing projects, and talking with students and colleagues about the heady world of ideas. What could be better?

Sure, sometimes grading papers is about as exciting as poking at my eyes with Q-tips. Some days, when students are tired and my own teaching runs flat, I think I would rather be working in an entirely different field: maybe as a dog walker, or as a famous TV script writer. A number of years ago, I complained to an officemate about how *hard* teaching first-year composition was, and he just guffawed. Right in my face. "You think this is hard?" he said. "Try working at a chicken packing plant for twelve-hour shifts. Or on a conveyer belt, stuffing some worthless trinket into plastic packaging." His perspective pulled me up short, and I've tried not to complain about the vagaries of teaching college students ever since.

This is not the narrative we are supposed to tell about our lives, though: that our jobs are easy, our schedules unpacked. Living the American dream means working hard, often far more than forty hours a week, because that's what is expected of us. In this case, being settled means being particularly unsettled, keeping a frenetic pace of work and life, and complaining consistently that we are overworked and tired. We've bought the lie, somehow, that being perpetually busy means being perpetually successful, and thus important. So most of us dive head-on into our work and families, knowing that the more we do, the more worthy others will deem us.

For several years, I had a friend whose response to "How are you doing?" was always—and I mean always—"I'm crazy busy." Her reply became predictable, and one she offered at every season, even though I knew there had to be moments when she was *not* crazy busy. What I heard in her "crazy busy" mantra was that she had no time for me or for our friendship, a subtext she may not have intended; in any case, I think having a full schedule made her feel important, made her feel worthy. Thanks to my former friend, in moments when I'm feeling particularly peevish, I respond to "How's life?" inquiries by saying "Not too exciting" or "Not much going on in my world," because this is *not* the response we are expected to give. Also, I never want to convey to others that I don't have time for them. Even this practice is difficult for me, though. I want others to find me worthy, and I know that my response makes it seem as though I'm not important enough to have a full schedule.

This expectation—that working hard makes us important— is embedded in the American dream, and the corollary expectation is that those who work hard will be rewarded. Our culture generally acknowledges those who have significant wealth as people who have worked hard and thus "deserve" their money and privilege. We often tell children that if they only work hard in school and in life, they will find success. I've been told that I deserve my tenure-track job and all its comforts because I worked hard in graduate school. But this rings hollow given the 60 percent of PhDs in my field who never find a tenured position—many of whom worked just as much, or more, than I did. And as my officemate reminded me, millions of folks toil at unfulfilling jobs, laboring harder than I do every day of the week, but who will never have the monetary resources I enjoy.

So, sure, most people are incredibly busy, given how fast-paced contemporary culture can be. Having a full-time job and ferrying my teenage sons to their activities can be taxing. But so can being the primary caregiver for young children, or caring for ailing parents, or being a single person who works extra hours to relieve colleagues with stress at home. The expectation that being busy connotes our worthiness means that we cannot ever rest, can never feel settled.

We lose a good deal when we expect people to be crazy busy, something to which my former friend can attest. Buying into the mythology that the worthy life is frenetic, we miss the opportunity to foster relationships with others, and also with ourselves. When we assume that a packed schedule reflects someone's significance, we convey that those who have space for leisure are less important, their time less valuable. We also lose capacity to be still and unoccupied, because that empty time feels worthless to us, despite what studies tell us about the need for silence, meditation, and unscheduled moments to relax.[10]

There will be times when circumstances will stretch our resources of time and energy. I think of friends who are caring for children with significant needs *and* parents with terminal illnesses. Of those who are working overtime because they are the sole breadwinners for a household, and doing anything less isn't possible right now. Of those who have three children under age three, for whom an entire night's rest is only a dream. They are busy people, for sure. But their worth is *still* not defined by what they do or how often they do it. They are inherently worthy, just as they are, in work and in rest—even if rest is in short supply right now.

BACK WHEN I WAS A SENIOR IN COLLEGE and a proposal from The One was not in the offing, I was certain that the good life was looming on the other side of commencement. A year later my one-year commitment in a voluntary service program was winding down, and I looked forward to moving nearer to home and to starting graduate school. I was eager to begin working toward my vocation as a teacher. And then I anticipated relocating for a doctoral program, excited for an adventure in a new state, with new people. After finishing my comprehensive exams and preparing for marriage, I knew that a spouse and a stable home on some property in Oregon would fulfill me—and it did, kind of, until a mouse infestation and land overrun by too many weeds compelled me to think that a house in town, on a smaller plot, would be great.

Having a career, having small children, having bigger children, having teenagers: at each phase of my life, I've believed that the *next* step will make me feel settled; I will finally feel that my life is enough. I am solidly middle-aged now, and I know I need to stop believing that the next stage in life is the one in which I will feel settled. At some point, there will be no next stage left.

The expectation of a good life waiting just around each corner is one I know many of us share. In part this seems like a survival mechanism, especially when where we are at is difficult. The promise of a more settled future can make the present more bearable. We also look around us—or, these days, log on to social media—and see others being settled in ways we are not. We hope that when we make some necessary changes in our lives, we will have what everyone else is having. That message of transformation is persistent in every stage of our lives, and the next big change we make will always be the one that finally, finally makes us feel fulfilled.

That's what the script for the settled life tells us, at any rate, informed by the sense that self-transformation is always necessary—that the world is expecting someone other than who we are right now. But I'm starting to recognize the flawed nature of this script. My resolution each New Year for the past decade or so has been to try my best to live in the moment rather than always projecting to some future time when I will be satisfied. (I recognize the irony of a resolution compelling me to be transformed in my own understanding of transformation.) I pray often that I will recognize the beauty of each moment, acknowledging as well that the moment is really all we have, the only time available to us to feel truly settled. I've also been getting therapy for a few years, working to feel satisfied in who God created me to be.

In *Traveling Mercies*, Anne Lamott writes about our longing for "permanence, a guarantee or two, the unconditional love we all long for," and the inability to receive what we desire. When reading Lamott, I often recognize that my desire to feel that I am enough, just as I am, is also this desire to feel unconditionally loved, to feel settled in my sense of self and my sense of worthiness. Lamott says she demands assurance from God that all will be well but gets only silence. And in that silence she realizes the only promise, the only thing in this life not shrouded by mystery, is "the moment, and the imperfect love of people."[11]

The imperfect love of people? That, it seems to me, is crucial, because those who have helped to create and reinforce the script of a perfectly settled life also have it in their power to change the script completely.

ALTHOUGH I CONSISTENTLY GRIPE about the ills of social media, one of the things I love is its ability to connect me with former students. In the days before Facebook, graduation often signaled the end of our relationship, save for Christmas cards and a now-and-then request to write recommendation letters. Now I can log on to Facebook or Instagram and see what these folks are up to, and I'm often thrilled by the beautiful lives my one-time charges have created. Some are marrying and starting families, for sure, but many are climbing mountains, traveling abroad, starting nonprofits, writing books, teaching others, and in other ways changing the world.

Posts on social media may at times remind us what a settled life is supposed to look like, with perfectly curated images showing us people who are happily coupled, happily parenting, happily succeeding at every business endeavor. Yet they can also suggest that other pathways are equally worthy to pursue. They allow us to celebrate people who are making different choices for their lives; they bear witness to a counternarrative, pushing back against all those pesky expectations that say you have to be married, or a parent, or busy, to be worthy. I imagine that if social media had existed back when I was younger and fretting about my own life as an unmarried woman, seeing others my age enjoying the single life might have changed everything, might have let me know that I was not alone in being alone. Who knows? If I hadn't felt so persistently that being happy meant being married, I could have spent my twenties through-hiking the Appalachian Trail or volunteering my time in India or, you know, even enjoying a bagel at the local bakery instead of eyeing every single man for potential spouse material. Knowing other people were out there, making bold choices about their lives, might have inspired me to find my own path as well.

Feeling less alone about the unique paths our lives can take does not necessarily require that we log on to social media, of course. We can also work to challenge those mythologies that tell people exactly what they *must* do to be considered worthy, and can celebrate each and every person's unique journey. This means stopping ourselves from assuming that marriage is the best gift God gives to everyone, and that those who are single have been denied this "blessing." This means refraining from judging those who are childfree, and affirming those whose families might not look like ours. This means honoring people who choose a slower life, and who make space for rest and reflection. (This might also mean allowing Netflix binging to be a valued pastime rather than a shameful secret.)

The imperfect love we have for each other, the imperfect love to which we are called, means that you will allow me to find my way, and that I will allow you to find yours, in a world where the script for our lives too often seems already written. Loving each other well means creating new scripts, no two alike, ones we are constantly writing and rewriting until the closing credits.

6

WHY MOWING THE LAWN CAN BE COMPLICATED

This first point is important to know: I had the best grandpa in the world.

Murray Springer lived his entire life in central Illinois, mostly in Hopedale, a small Mennonite farming community near Peoria. He was a foreman for the Caterpillar tractor company and worked the night shift. By the time I came around, he was retired, spending his mornings drinking coffee uptown and his afternoons drinking beer in his garage. He was what people might call a "man's man," someone who enjoyed Kool cigarettes, Schlitz beer from a can, and the World Wrestling Federation on television. He was a fan of boxing and Smokin' Joe Frazier. He loved meat and potatoes.

When I was a girl, Murray Springer, the best grandpa in the world, was my hero. And this made the lesson I learned from him about gender roles even more difficult to bear.

As a ten-year-old, I idolized my grandpa so much that I requested a pair of bib overalls for my birthday so I could match my grandpa's wardrobe. He'd give me his old Dekalb Seed caps, which I wore with the bill tilted slightly to the right, just like Grandpa. The smell of his sweaty bald head lingered in the hat's mesh, and when I'd go home after a visit, I could inhale the sweat-and-cigarette fragrance of the cap and be transported back to Hopedale and the best grandpa in the world.

In the summer, my siblings and I spent one or two weeks in Hopedale, giving my parents a respite. Our grandparents' small house was an oasis, with sugared cereal every breakfast, an unlimited supply of popsicles, an ample yard for Wiffle ball games, and, for me, hours of hanging out with Grandpa. He and I sat out in the garage in matching lawn chairs, drinking from the beverage cans he stored in the extra refrigerator: Schlitz for him, Shasta cream soda for me. Some days I'd ride along while he did chores for his farmer friends, sitting in the front seat of his Chevy, each of us with an arm crooked out an open window.

We were compadres, my grandpa and me . . . until it came time for my grandparents to dole out chores. Then Grandpa would send me into the kitchen to help my grandma with meal preparation, and he'd call my brother outside to mow the yard, help him in the garden, or pick up sticks around the big oak tree. I'd go inside begrudgingly, never happy to be confined in the air-conditioned house knowing my Dekalb Seed cap and bib overalls were irrelevant for the kind of work I'd be doing.

Don't get me wrong: I loved my grandma. But I didn't feel especially suited to the chores she wanted me to do. While I snapped green beans with Grandma at the kitchen sink, I could see my brother's dour face, now puffy with allergies, riding the lawnmower back and forth across my grandparents' vast yard. It didn't make sense to me. I wanted so badly to be outside, working with Grandpa, doing physical labor in the hot sun, and I knew my brother much preferred being inside with Grandma, where the air was always cooler and the television always on.

This was my first lesson in gender inequity. Girls did *not* do heavy labor, including mowing the lawn. Boys who chose to work in the kitchen were sissies, no matter their personal preference or how much they loved watching *As the World Turns* every afternoon at one o'clock Central. I don't blame my grandparents for their entrenched beliefs. My grandparents grew up in a different time and lived in a small midwestern town where traditional gender roles were never questioned.

Some believe that this sense of specific gender roles is anachronistic and that girls and boys learn today that they can be whatever they long to be. To some extent, this is true. More than ever before, girls are allowed to dream big about their vocations—much bigger than I could even thirty years ago, when my announcement to a classmate that I wanted to be a farmer was met with a smirk. A farmer's wife, maybe. But the one running the machinery, strong-arming livestock, driving the combine? Not likely.

We've come a long way, baby. Today, young women graduate from college at rates higher than their male peers, and are just as likely to enter occupations that were once dominated by men. A 2014 report by the White House Council of Economic Advisers showed that women are becoming doctors, lawyers, and business administrators at the same rate as they are assuming jobs as teachers, nurses, or administrative assistants, roles traditionally considered more suitable for women.[1] Similarly, men are taking on roles that would have at one time been considered too feminine. Nursing programs have an increasing number of male students, and more men than ever before are choosing to be elementary teachers. (Never mind that a disparity in earning means that women's paychecks are still smaller than those of men in similar positions doing similar work.[2])

We might be inclined to believe that the glass ceiling has truly been dismantled and that our daughters can assume and excel at any vocation they choose. For many people in the United States, the 2016 presidential election—the first in which a woman ran as a major party presidential candidate—proved once and for all that gender discrimination is a thing of past. For others, Hillary Clinton's loss to Donald Trump signaled that sexism is alive and well.

Many people no longer fret over concerns about clearly defined gender roles. If he were alive today, Murray Springer might be able to see how silly it was to make his granddaughter snap beans when she clearly preferred mowing the yard. The fact that my sons recognize lawn mowing as a chore their mom nearly always does suggests we don't automatically assume there are substantially different roles for men and women in private and public life.

Yet in many Christian circles, the mythology persists that God assigns different roles to men and women—not only assigns these roles, but also demands that people remain within them no matter their gifting or their interests. This mythology undergirds much of Christian culture's teaching about the place women can have in leadership, and it compels a good number of churches to assert that women cannot serve as church leaders, because doing so would transgress God's design for women's lives. The myth about God's design for women and men shapes the ways we talk about marriage and family and distorts the ways both men and women relate to God and to each other. It creates cognitive dissonance for young people who struggle to reconcile what they see as their calling with what they hear from Christian leaders.

More than that, though, this idea of "God's design" means that many people, both women and men, are funneled into molds that fit uncomfortably, if at all. The idea also sets up expectations that cannot always be met and leads to moments of real despair for those who cannot fill the roles they've supposedly been designed to fill. This can cause acute feelings of unworthiness. Finding ourselves in a world expecting someone else means acknowledging that gender does not always determine one's calling. It means challenging systems and institutions that codify gender injustice, in North America and around the world. It means creating a different world, one where women and men truly are free to be who and what God intended.

I REMEMBER EXACTLY WHERE I WAS when I decided to play middle school football. Fifth and sixth graders in Hillsboro were bused ten miles away to Durham each day, and once, on the way back from our daily trip through Kansas wheat fields, I announced to the kids sitting next to me that I would be trying out for football in the fall instead of volleyball. Maybe I'd had an especially inspired day in phys ed class, serving on the offensive line for our flag football team and blocking the girls on the other side so that Mike, our quarterback, could make a long pass before getting his flag ripped from his belt. Mike always played quarterback, of course, because he was blond, handsome, athletic, and the alpha male of sixth grade.

The other guys served as receivers, and girls took the less glam-
orous roles. Apparently I thought that if I could play football
during class, I might as well try out for the team. And so, on
a bus grinding its gears toward Hillsboro, I let others know
about my ambitions.

"Yeah, right," Lane said, his prepubescent lip curling into a
sneer. "That's dumb."

"No, it's not," I insisted. Hadn't he seen the way I pushed
Laurie so hard off the front line that she'd cried? Didn't he see
her slump to the sideline, claiming my block had somehow
broken her glasses? Didn't this prove I was tough enough?

"Girls don't play football," Lane said. The clump of boys
sitting behind him laughed in agreement. "What an idiot."

I wanted to tell him *he* was the idiot, and that girls do play
football. But I knew at some level that trying out for the middle
school team was foolhardy. The next fall, I'd be wearing those
awful polyester volleyball uniforms with too-tight shorts and
silly looking knee pads, trying not to panic every time a ball
was served toward my head. My desire to put on a helmet and
tackle some kids would never be realized. Lane was right: girls
did not play football. At least not when it mattered.

By the time I was twelve, I had already internalized messages about what was possible for me as a girl and what was
not. I also knew that girls were not worth as much as boys and
that boys would always get to do more fun, more challenging,
more adventurous stuff, just because. These messages came not
from my parents, both of whom were fairly progressive and
wanted their daughters to dream big. Instead, I had learned
from my community, my culture, my extended family, and my
church what girls should not do, given their biological design,
their weaker bodies, and their presumably natural inclinations.

In this regard, not much has changed. Girls still don't go out for football—or, the girls who do are lionized in the media as bizarre freaks of nature. There are semiprofessional organizations for women who play football, but until 2013, this league was called the "Lingerie Football League" and women wore bikini panties and bras under their shoulder pads.

So yes, even though there is growing equity in the professional roles men and women enter, great disparity remains. We generally assume that some jobs are more suitable for men and some jobs more suitable for women. Indeed, we need look no further than politics in the United States to see how firmly we have accepted the mythology that men are naturally inclined to be strong leaders and that women—given their tendency to be emotive and their desire to be peacemakers—will not be as successful. Why has it taken until 2016 for a woman to be nominated for president by a major party? Whether we want to admit it or not, voting for a woman in leadership means fighting against the presumption that women are not natural leaders. This is especially true in Christian circles. In the run-up to the 2016 presidential election, a number of websites were considering the quandary in which white evangelical Christians found themselves: should they vote for a presumably ungodly man, like Donald Trump, or a woman, Hillary Clinton?

Although many evangelical Christian voters claimed they supported Trump because of his pro-life platform, many also couldn't bring themselves to vote for a woman as a leader of the most powerful nation in the world, since God had not designed women to lead. In postmortems of the 2016 election, pollsters discovered that a majority of white women voted for Trump, even after the candidate was caught boasting about actions that amounted to sexual assault. Although many of these voters said they chose the Republican candidate because of his anti-abortion platform and his economic policies, they were also electing a man who said that women who had been harassed on the job should simply find another job—if women even should be working at all.[3]

Christians who believe strongly in God's specific design for men and women will point to the first chapters of Genesis, asserting that Eve was created from Adam's rib as a helpmeet. God's creative act puts men in charge, with women serving as their helpers and taking on roles that originally allowed Adam to do the hard work of tending a garden, naming every species of animal, and being the provider. Some Christians argue that this reflects men's natural tendency toward operating in the public sphere, and that Adam, being initially a perfect reflection of God's image, had the strength and capabilities necessary to be a leader—as does every man who has followed, given that he is a son of Adam.

Those daughters of Eve? As the first woman, crafted from the rib of Adam, and given the role of helping her spouse, Eve provides the model for every woman born thereafter. Even the physical design of women, it is argued, reflects this theory. Women are less strong than men, less able to be providers or hunters and gatherers, built rather to be nurturers of others. This, some who believe in "God's design" might say, was written right into Adam and Eve's DNA.

This particular understanding of "God's design" is complicated by many Christians' affirmation that God *did* design the world through God's creative act and then called it good. Is it possible to hold in tension this sense that God designed my intricate body, gendered female by my DNA, as well as the belief that this gendering does not necessarily determine what roles I can play in my personal and professional life? According to complementarian theology, "God's design" insists that both are intricately linked and that *because of* God's creation of my XX chromosomes—my imprint as a daughter of Eve—I am designed to assume a specific place in my world, even if that place doesn't specifically suit me.

Some Christians assume a different posture toward gender roles, one that nonetheless lands at the same complementarian ideology: God desires specific and compatible but distinct roles for men and women to be maintained, thanks to the fall. In Genesis 2, this line of thinking goes, both Adam and Eve played the same roles in the garden because God made men and women equal in all things. Then Eve bungled things up by making sure Adam ate from the tree of knowledge. Thus, while it's not God's *will* that men and women take on different roles, what can you do? The fall has messed up everything, sin runs rampant, and as a result, boys get to play football while girls are consigned to wearing polyester volleyball shorts.

Those who perpetuate the myth of gender roles assume that this understanding of gender is inviolate. Even men's and women's bodies, they say, demonstrate that we are supposed to assume different roles in the world. The "God's design" folks will show how a woman's uterus and breasts mean that she is built primarily to birth children and nurture them and that men, with their stronger physiques, are created to go out into the world to provide for women. For some, this physical manifestation of God's intentions for women and men is also written into their internal wiring. According to John Eldredge, author of the popular book *Wild at Heart*, men are encoded with the desire to pursue princesses, to embrace their own warrior spirits, and to be providers and protectors and leaders.

This wild heart might be battered by contemporary culture's insistence that men be emotive and relational, Eldredge asserts, but buried deep inside, beneath the culture's emasculating detritus, a warrior stands at the ready. Real men, godly men, will peel back that effeminate shell to find their true, divinely designed selves, and all will be right with the world.

Eldredge published *Wild at Heart* in 2001; a companion book for women, called *Captivating* (published with Eldredge's spouse, Stasi), continued the theme of God's design, letting women know that their own hearts have been distorted by those who would want them to be equal to men. Women don't actually want to be strong, independent leaders, the Eldredges believe. Instead, women long to be pursued by their warriors, to be cared for, to be treated like the princesses they are certainly designed to be. Contemporary culture—what with its attempts to give women equality with men—has tamped the desires of women's hearts way, way down deep.

The impact of the Eldredges' theory about gender—for it is only a theory, after all—cannot be understated. Their books have fueled an entire industry of Christian products designed to help women and men discover their true, God-given roles, roles the Eldredges believe have been so obliterated by contemporary culture as to be unrecognizable. The millions of Christians who have taken the Eldredges' message to heart hear that these theories are, in fact, biblical, and that more than anything else, God longs for men to be warriors and women to be princesses. The Eldredges' ability to perpetuate the myth of God-sanctified gender roles would be laughable save for this enormous influence.

When I think about the men in my life, it's hard for me to find a warrior among them. Perhaps my work in an English department somehow shields me from knowing true war-rior-men. My male colleagues, whom I love and admire deeply, are more inclined to spend a quiet evening at home reading Thoreau or C. S. Lewis than to run through the woods to find their warrior hearts. I've also never fancied my husband, a ter-rific father and loving partner, as a wild-at-heart man, machete raised, ready to massacre anything that stands in the way of his finding his princess. And me as a princess, waiting in the high-est turret for him to arrive? Laughable. I'd probably wonder what the heck was taking him so long, and why he got to have all the fun, running through the woods.

Now, it could be that my decidedly unwarrior-like colleagues are deluding themselves, and that I am as well. It could be that we have all buried our true natures so deeply that the very idea of becoming a warrior—or a princess—is inconceivable. John Eldredge would like us to believe this: that the essence of who men and women are, given their different genders, has been obfuscated by feminists who want to make everyone equal. In this view, feminists have worked hard to destroy the very traits that make women's specific roles so special, so necessary to the kingdom, so distinct from the roles given to men.

Or it could be that the very idea of gender roles is based on contemporary cultural stereotypes about men and women, dealing less with biological determinism and more with the ways Eldredge et al. would like people to be. Because when we say that all men are wild at heart, and all women long to be captivating, we begin to shove people into molds that might well fit uncomfortably, no matter their XX or XY chromo-somes. We also make people aware of their inherent unwor-thiness if they don't want to be warriors or princesses, letting them know there is something wrong with *them* rather than with the *Wild at Heart* theology that demands all women, and all men, be exactly the same.

BACK WHEN I WAS TWELVE and dreaming of being a football player or a farmer, I didn't realize that farming was part of my heritage, a lineage that ran through my mother's family. My grandma herself had been a farmer, long before I was born. My maternal grandfather, Theodore Schmidt, farmed near Goessel, Kansas, growing wheat and raising live-stock until his untimely death at fifty-nine, when my mom, the youngest of five, was a first-year student in college. For a time after his death, my grandma Mary continued to operate the farm, taking on the many jobs her husband once did. Those who embrace an understanding of God's design for men and women would say that she was not suited to be a farmer and that she should not have taken on roles reserved for men. But she *had* to assume chores; she had no other choice.

This is also lost in the "God's design" debates: when people talk about God-created gender roles, they are doing so from a place of privilege—one that says women choose to operate in the public sphere and that those making the choice to work out-side the home are not following the desire of God's heart. This privilege was most obvious to me when I became a working mother, my radar finely attuned to those who argue that women should stay home and act as nurturers, the number one role for which God had designed them. One Tuesday, after picking up my son from my mother's (where he spent every Tuesday while I worked), I was listening to the Dr. Laura show on the radio. I listened to Dr. Laura religiously, even if I didn't buy into her religion; it was my own form of masochism, I'm sure.

At any rate, Dr. Laura was castigating yet another mom who was working outside the home, letting her know she needed to quit her job immediately. When the mother said the family relied on her income, Dr. Laura began berating the woman's husband, whom she saw as an unfit provider. The husband needed to take on two or three jobs, however many necessary, so that the woman could stay home, Dr. Laura said; only then would they be fulfilling their proper roles. Only then would they be happy. Even though I was tapped out from working full-time and caring for my kid, I knew Dr. Laura's advice seemed silly and narrow-minded. Why was it solely a man's responsibility to provide for a family, especially if that meant he worked multiple jobs and never saw his children? This seemed unfair to him, putting on him not only the onus of providing, but also the costs in terms of separation from his kids.

As I immersed myself in Christian culture, though, studying this idea of God's design, I learned that Dr. Laura's advice was fairly mainstream and that many Christians believed women should assume the role of nurturer for the family, and men the role of provider. Not only was this view widespread, it was also based on several assumptions: That women always had spouses who could work outside the home. That men could always find jobs, or several jobs, to support a family. That women were far better than men at taking care of children, and men far better at being providers. Imagine, then, what a single mother must hear when she is told that God has designed her to nurture her children but not support them. Or when a father who delights in spending time with his children learns that he needs to work several jobs to provide for his family, giving him little time to see his kids develop. He may also learn he is a poor provider, and thus ungodly, because he needs so many jobs to make ends meet. Both women and men who operate outside the stipulations of this paradigm may feel inherently unworthy, challenged to live in roles for which they are poorly equipped.

This idea of God's design also does not consider the ways women throughout history have been integrally involved in the work of tending livestock, raising crops, working in factories. It is Western-focused, and it neglects the fact that throughout the world, women work outside the home, often by necessity. In times of war especially, when men left for the battlefield and casualties decimated the workforce, women stepped into jobs normally considered "men's work." During the Civil War and the First and Second World Wars, women worked in industry and on farms. While visiting India a few years ago, I saw countless women hauling bricks for construction, toiling in the hot Delhi sun to build sidewalks. This kind of work was probably not their ideal, but I imagine they had little other choice. Although some Christians would certainly argue that their need to work outside the home doing heavy labor is a result of the fall and sin's entry in the world, such claims feel disingenuous. That's because the argument changes shape when considering women in the United States, where men are told, à la Dr. Laura, to do everything in their powers to keep women in their "designed" role. This assertion is incredibly weighted by privilege and assumes that God's design applies only to those in Western countries, not to women in other parts of the world.

If that's the case, can it really be God's design at all? Or is it just one more way that Christian culture tries to keep a woman in a carefully proscribed role, letting her know she's unworthy of exploring her own unique calling?

RIGHT BEFORE I ENTERED NINTH GRADE, my family moved from Hillsboro, Kansas, to Albany, Oregon. My dad assumed a new pastoral role at a Mennonite church in Albany. I don't know if my dad really knew how much more conservative our new church was until we were already planted in Albany, living in a too-small house while my mom pined for the expansive parsonage we'd left behind.

Our new church had very particular views about women in leadership positions, making it clear that women were designed by God to teach other women and children, make coffee, and organize meals when needed. Early in my dad's tenure in the church, we met Lois, a fiery, outspoken woman who clearly had gifts in leadership—gifts she used to manage a large strawberry farm but that could not be called upon in the church. I remember Lois as a diminutive woman with a loud voice, a person I both admired and feared (the latter mostly because I was an inept strawberry picker, and when I was under her employ she sometimes chastised me for leaving too many ripe berries to rot). But I also respected Lois's passion for peacemaking and her persistent witness in church about justice. It was a witness that Lois could never share from the pulpit, since that was not a space where women could stand, figuratively or literally. At the church where my dad pastored, and at countless churches still, Christians hew closely to the words set forth in 1 Timothy 2, where Paul writes, "I permit no woman to teach or have authority over a man; she is to keep silent." Although many Christians read this passage within its historical context and within the context of Paul's other writings, a number still interpret this as God throwing down his order that women remain silent. Paul has been used as a fine surgical tool for removing women's voices and for compelling churches to split hairs about what women can and cannot do solely because of their gender.

This meant that Lois—fearless, articulate, passionate Lois—could speak to her congregation, but only from the floor of the sanctuary, not from behind the pulpit. Talk about sticking to the letter of the law but not its spirit! The church's elders let her know that her voice mattered, but less than that of *any* man in the church, who could pull himself up from the wooden benches and proceed to the pulpit to read Scripture, make announcements, share prayer concerns. It didn't matter what he said, because he was a man, and thus designed by God to speak truths in the ways even the most gifted woman could not.

My church was not unusual in this kind of hairsplitting, and other women have told me stories about the ways their congregations chose to divine what Paul was writing about in 1 Timothy 2: They could speak from a music stand, but not a pulpit. They could speak at Sunday or Wednesday night services, but not on Sunday mornings. They could teach Sunday school to children (boy, could they ever do that!), but they could not teach Sunday school to adults, or at least not adults who were men. They could preach at women-only conferences, but if the audience was mixed-gender, a man also needed to be part of the stage, exerting his authority over the gathering.

The truth is, this idea of silence and God's design for women has been used for generations to keep women silent. If a woman wants to speak, she has very few avenues within the church to do so, and must always wonder whether what she is doing matches her "design" or whether it is somehow outside of God's will. At times, this demand that women remain muted has come at great cost to women, especially those who have experienced abuse and who are told that silence is the appropriate response to male power. Women's silence in the face of assault is one of many outcomes of this message that a woman's voice is not as valuable as a man's. There are cases at Christian universities where female students, having reported their abuse to administrators, are disciplined for "fornicating" or are not believed or are told that staying silent about assault might be the best, most godly thing they can do.[4] Other church organizations and denominations have also kept women silent in the face of abuse, believing—implicitly, at least—that women had no voice in the church. Attempts to silence women's voices—and assertions that such silencing is biblical—are one more way we have told women that their experiences are not worthy, even when those experiences are traumatic and life-changing. Saving men's reputations and the reputations of the institutions they represent seems to matter so much more.

IT HAPPENS EVERY SEMESTER: a student comes into my office, feeling angst about her calling and about what her parents and her conservative culture have told her she should be. Often these conversations turn tearful as the student expresses real conflict about what her evangelical upbringing taught her and what she is experiencing in college. Through their time at George Fox, students discover they have agency, voices, and vocations, which is exactly what a liberal arts college should be teaching them. Many students have grown up learning that women need to remain silent, passive, and focused on becoming wives and mothers. This dissonance creates inner turmoil for students, who come to faculty offices expressing a desire to follow their callings but who also believe their vocational aspirations might be against God's will.

So my female students wonder: Could they really be pastors and church leaders, even though the Bible—or, really, a specific reading of the Bible—had told them women should remain silent? Could they forego marriage and motherhood, at least for a while, to pursue a career, even though they were told that being a wife and mother was their highest calling? How could they square what they were beginning to believe with what they had been told the Bible says? It is all so confusing, so disruptive to their sense of self.

One of the distinct messages people hear about God's design for gender is that any calling which runs counter to that design must be sublimated. A woman who feels called to church leadership isn't hearing God correctly; she must be seeking a position as lead pastor because of selfish conceit. Countless evangelical leaders have made this point clear: churches that allow women to preach are not following God's Word but their own wisdom. These churches are not biblical. They will face consequences for going against what God has commanded.

Of course, this ideology is shifting in many Western churches, and many women are fully supported in finding their vocations outside any notion of "God's design." And yet a large number of churches—including the Roman Catholic Church, the largest Western church body—still affirm the beliefs that women cannot serve from the pulpit and that God has designed women and men for distinct, special roles. The reverberations of this idea are significant and can be seen in the relative absence of women in leadership roles for our para-church organizations, our Christian institutions, our Fortune 500 companies, our government offices. Some people defend this dearth of leadership by noting that women often make the intentional choice of family over career advancement and thus are less likely to ascend to higher ranks in any company, organization, or government. This rationale seems problematic for sure, because it reflects and reinforces a foundational belief that women are not designed to lead, that their voices are not designed to speak with authority, and that men will always do better in these roles.

In this, popular culture and Christian culture have colluded to give women and men consistent messages about who and what they are to be, solely on the basis of their gender. From an early age, we are bombarded with images everywhere about what women can do because of their "design." When Barbie proclaims she is bad at math; when Legos "for girls" are pink and marketed as beauty salons; when parents themselves are two and a half times more likely to wonder whether their boys are gifted geniuses than their girls: when all these messages converge on us from our infancy, we are likely to believe that gender roles are inherently responsible for the ways we think, act, and even emote. In recent studies, children as young as seven associate intelligence with boys far more than with girls. Lin Bian, a psychologist at the University of Illinois, found that girls were also far more reluctant to play games meant for "really smart people." This sense that brilliance and genius are specifically masculine traits persists into adulthood, with studies showing that a majority of men believe their intelligence is higher than it really is, whereas women rate their intelligence lower than it is in actuality. Messages about the abilities of men and women have significant consequences. Bian concludes, "In the long-term it will steer away many young women from careers that are thought to require brilliance."[5]

Here's the truth: mass media has compelled us to believe the lie that women are only good at some activities and that men are good at an entirely different set. Christian culture has taken this ideology one step further, telling us that these differences are part of God's grand design. Images that go against this dominant narrative are lauded as edgy or as exceptions that prove the rule. The cereal commercial featuring a dad and his daughter is amazing because it shows the dad getting breakfast for his kid. Casting a woman in a role as a construction worker is amazing because it shows a woman doing something outside of what's expected. A woman assuming the helm of a Fortune 500 company is celebrated because this is so far beyond of what women normally do. Both Christian and popular culture peddle stereotypes, reinforcing our sense that women and men who step outside some kind of divinely endorsed "role" are outliers going against either what mass media expects or what God has sanctified.

So how do we find ourselves in a world where gender roles are still so deeply entrenched? I mean that question in two ways: What are we still doing here, in the twenty-first century, where women have made so many gains but have yet to find equity? How do we find ourselves in a world where, in some places, even little girls getting an education can seem like a threat? But the question also challenges us to consider how we discover our God-given gifts, as women *and* men, when our cultures tell us that our vocations, our skills, our life paths must be determined more by gender than by anything else.

Growing up, my heroes were women who pushed against gendered stereotypes, who defied barriers to their becoming fully who they want to be. I admired those women who transgressed even the smallest of gender norms, because they served as a model of possibility, letting me know that being a woman did not have to limit me. I remember well the church camp counselors who talked about college as if it was absolutely normal for women to get an education. The women in my church, those who grasped whatever leadership roles they could, brushing against the stained glass ceilings of our religious communities. A college professor who unabashedly modeled for me what life might look like as a working mother. A graduate school administrator who stood up against a misogynistic faculty colleague on my behalf, letting him know that the leering invitations to his office were a gross misuse of power. Again and again, I've had women open a different world for me, one where we—as women with voices, minds, agency—could find ourselves.

One way we claim our God-created selves in a gendered world, then, is to be models and mentors who point to another way of operating in the workplace, in schools, and in our homes. When my kids were toddlers, I brought them to campus regularly. There were few other mothers in faculty roles on campus, and I wanted my students to see that women could be good mothers and good professionals, and that the possibility of being one did not exclude the possibility of another. Other women have similarly served as mentors to me, helping me navigate a tenure review process that seemed, at the time, more an old boys' network than an equitable path to promotion. Even as I've grown older and sometimes wondered whether having a mentor might still be necessary, I've found courage and strength from younger women, too, whose wisdom and life experience has given me direction I sometimes didn't know I needed. Some women and men, standing aside and letting me use my own voice, have helped me find courage to speak about gender injustice in my church and at my workplace.

Yes, I mean women *and* men. When we talk about gender injustice, too often it's assumed that women want to dominate men or that they want to create a society in which men get their comeuppance after centuries of domination. Perhaps there are feminists who believe this. Most of us who claim a feminist identity, however, do so because we embrace what's at the heart of feminist ideology: that we are all created equal and that we can all rise together once we destroy the systems and the ideologies that dictate one gender's superiority over another. *We all rise together*: that sensibility allows us to claim that we are all worthy, no matter one's gender.

I want to believe that if my grandparents were alive today, they might have let me drive the riding lawnmower and invited my brother inside to help Grandma with dinner. It's easy to imagine a different childhood, one where I maneuvered that Snapper mower around Grandpa's ample yard, my Dekalb hat tilted over my curly hair; given how much better of a cook my brother still is, I can easily imagine him sitting alongside Grandma, learning our family recipes. We found ourselves in a different world growing up, one that saw our gender more than our gifts or inclinations, and my childhood memories are colored by the many times my brother experienced a life I wanted for myself, but couldn't have as a girl.

That's not a world I want for my kids, for my students, for myself. I want my boys to find themselves in a different world, one where they see possibility everywhere. Fortunately, given their parents, their church environment, and their school culture, this is the case. I have hope they will believe—really believe—that they can do anything they feel called to do. Because my students' church and family cultures are often more conservative than the one I've cultivated for my family,

I know it's up to me and my colleagues to encourage young women and men to pursue vocational goals dependent not on their gender but on God's good and rich calling. I have faith in my colleagues and in our institution that this can happen, especially when we work to push back against gender stereotypes.

We all have it in our power to find ourselves in a different world, one where girls can mow the yard—or play football, or speak in church, or get an education, or find their voices. And where they will feel, truly feel, that these endeavors are not so complicated after all.

7

HAIR (AND A THIGH GAP) MAKES A GIRL

The first time I got kicked out of a women's restroom, I was twelve years old.

At halftime of a basketball game we were watching, my friends and I had bought candy from the concession stand and made a stop at the bathroom. My friends got far enough into the restroom to enter empty stalls. I did not. As I walked in, a group of cheerleaders told me I was clearly in the wrong space and I had better scram, since I was obviously a boy—and a perverted one at that, trying to get a peek of women peeing. I slipped out of the restroom without my friends knowing, my face burning with shame.

Over the next decade, getting banished from women's restrooms happened frequently, and I developed strategies to avoid that particular humiliation: not peeing until I got home, or surrounding myself with girls who could vouch for my gender, or—at least two or three times—capitulating completely and going into men's rooms just to save myself from other kinds of embarrassment. Even now, several decades after the last time I was mistaken for a man, my heart still clenches momentarily when I go into a public restroom. The sting of my earlier shame is a constant reminder that, for years, people assumed I was a boy and that I had nefarious reasons for seeking out women-only spaces.

My mortification extended beyond being expelled from bathrooms. Teachers puzzled over my name on class rosters, wondering why the boy standing before them answered to a girl's name. At more than one athletic competition, a coach second-guessed my gender, accusing me of trying to get a competitive advantage by entering a girls-only race. As a first-year student at a Christian college, I was occasionally banished from women's dormitories, including my own, for transgressing "floor hour" rules about men being on women's dorm floors. I could catalog dozens of instances when I was humiliated by someone who looked at my physical appearance and decided I was not the girl (or woman) I claimed to be.

The most embarrassing confrontations occurred when I was with others—like the time when, at eighteen, I was at the state fair with friends, wearing platter-sized earrings and trying hard to appear feminine. A group of teenage boys swaggered toward us and announced I was the ugliest guy they'd ever seen. I wanted to die—literally, not figuratively. After this and other encounters, I wondered how hard it would actually be to drive my car off the road and end my life.

Some people might wonder why I didn't just try to look more feminine to preserve myself from heartache. Here are the reasons I offer: In a time before good hair products could control curly hair, I kept mine cut short, hoping to limit the wild frizz. I sometimes wore my brother's hand-me-downs because my dad was not fairly compensated as a pastor and we couldn't always afford new clothes. I was a late bloomer with a flat chest and an athletic build, and I felt more comfortable in jeans and tennis shoes.

Here is what I don't say: in my appearance, I was trying to align my inside with my outside, and my inside never felt comfortable in frills and lace, even when my culture insisted that this is what every girl would want to wear.

Most people looked at me and saw someone not pretty enough, feminine enough, or shapely enough to be a girl. After more than a decade of hearing that being myself meant not being recognized as a woman, what I learned—what I internalized—was that my body was to be reviled rather than accepted. I also learned I would never be enough, given my body shape and size, the curl of my hair, and my unwillingness to capitulate to societal standards about what it meant to look like a woman.

I now fit those standards more closely, thanks mostly to longer hair, a softer face, and a willingness to wear clothes that more closely approximate my culture's definition of feminine. Yet the damage has been done. When I am in a group of female friends, or standing in front of my classrooms, or sitting across the table from my husband, or wearing a swimsuit, I still struggle to accept this female body I've been given. I still wonder what it really feels like to be feminine.

I still believe I am not enough.

ALTHOUGH MY EXPERIENCE MIGHT BE UNIQUE, the truth is that we all receive plenty of complicated messages about our embodied selves. We all face expectations about what our bodies should look like and how they are to be inhabited. Those expectations come from multiple sources and at every stage in our life journey, to the point that it seems unlikely that most of us will ever feel as if our bodies live up to the expectations established for us. It's little wonder that most people report great dissatisfaction with their bodies and that, if given the opportunity, most would seek to make one or more changes to some aspect of their human form.

The diet and beauty industry is fueled by our body hatred and our longing to look like someone else. In one recent study, eight out of ten women surveyed felt that they were in the "wrong" body.[1] Christian culture has done little to assuage our discomfort with our bodies, setting up expectations about modesty, purity, sex, and sexuality that often make people, especially women, feel shame about their bodies. Sometimes we might even believe that feeling shame is exactly what we *should* do, given the stories we've heard about the garden of Eden and the fall. Our bodily shame is an inherited reaction to Adam and Eve's disobedience in the garden.

We rarely analyze this interpretation of Genesis or push back against the messages about our bodies. Instead, we swallow them whole, then spend our lifetimes trying to change the bodies we've been given, to make them more acceptable, more worthy. Every now and then, I can acknowledge the wasted time I've spent longing for a new body rather than the one I've grown into. But then I slip back into old patterns, the entrenched messages rattling around in my mind like a bad radio station, telling me my body has never been good enough, feminine enough, thin enough, beautiful enough, just as it is. I would be willing to bet that most women in Western culture, and quite a few men, are tapped into the same channel.

That station played its loudest in my head several years ago when I tried taking Zumba classes for a few months. As someone who never danced much, I envied those in the classes whose hips could move with ease. I looked at my friends who smiled and swung their bodies back and forth, sensuously grooving to the music, and felt only mortification at my own stiff hips, the awkward jolting motion I made, the grim concentration I needed to sway my booty, even a little bit. After many classes, I cried alone in my car, embarrassed by my inhibition, humiliated by my body.

I longed to be different, to be like my friends, dancing freely in bodies they seemed to accept. Every once in a while, through my tears, I would recall an essay in Anne Lamott's *Traveling Mercies*, where she describes watching a documentary film about several elderly women dancing joyfully on screen without much inhibition, despite their aging bodies. Rather than feeling encumbered or self-conscious, the women move gracefully, lacking fear or restraint. And Lamott, hyperaware of the extra weight she is carrying and her middle-aged sagginess, sees in the women a model for her own aspiration: to shrug off cultural expectations about her appearance and simply dance. She writes, "Coming out of the movie that night, I realized that I want what the crones have: time for all those long deep breaths, time to watch more closely, time to learn to enjoy what I've always been afraid of—the sag and the invisibility, the ease of understanding that life is not about doing. . . . What I am going to do instead is to begin practicing cronehood as soon as possible: to watch, smile, dance."[2]

Like Lamott, I want to claim what those older women have, smiling and dancing without fear. I would love for all the messages I've internalized about my embodied self to vanish so that I can dance without shame, embracing the sensuality of my middle-aged self, celebrating the good fortune of having a healthy body for nearly fifty years.

To dance would also mean to accept the amazing unique-ness of my body, both its strengths and its limitations. To dance would mean deciding that, despite the many expectations I have failed to meet, my body is worthy. It would mean finding and embracing myself, just the way God created me.

ABOUT FOUR YEARS AGO, I joined a gym in town, finally convinced I need to lift weights to keep osteoporosis at bay and to tone up my increasingly wobbly arms. Even though I'd been a runner for going on thirty-five years, joining a gym seemed incredibly risky; I was certain I'd feel out of place with all the young, lithe, blond women I knew would be there, wearing the latest Lululemon workout wear. Advertisements and fitness magazines had assured me that women who exercised in gym settings fit a certain image, one to which my own body did not conform, ever.

At the first group fitness experience, though, I discovered my prejudices about gym members to be unfounded. Every woman in that class—including the instructor—seemed entirely normal. The class faced a mirror for its entirety, and as someone who was taught humility as a virtue, watching myself work out was a challenge. Nonetheless, in that class, as in every other I attended, I have loved looking at the women exercising around me. Some days, during a particularly hard set of bicep curls or lunges, I feel in awe of the beauty I see in the mirror, reflecting the strength of these women, their willingness to push themselves, the exquisite diversity in their bodies, which come in all shapes, ages, and sizes.

Being able to see beauty in every body and in one's self, which is a harder task, takes a paradigm shift, to be sure. Our expectations about our bodies are shaped not by reality but by popular culture, including advertisers who tell us what we should hate about our bodies and what needs to be changed for our bodies to be deemed worthy. We assume this standard to be inviolate, rarely considering that our understanding of what makes a body beautiful is culturally driven. And even when we know that the standard for beauty *is* driven by advertisers wanting to sell us products, shifting our perspective can be extraordinarily difficult. Resistance seems mostly futile, and even now—more even than when I was twelve, or sixteen, or twenty—I feel compelled to change my body. These days I feel that I need to erase evidence of middle age, as a youthful body is what my culture suggests I inhabit, else I become invisible and thus unworthy.

According to Amanda Scherker, writing for the Huffington Post, the very fact that we are generally appalled by body hair on women is thanks to advertisers, who have convinced us that a hairless body on women is more attractive, more feminine.[3] Indeed, advertisers have driven many of our expectations about what makes a body worthy, and we are told our hair shouldn't be too gray; our skin shouldn't be too pale (unless you are a racial minority, in which case your skin shouldn't be too dark); our natural scent shouldn't be too strong, and should be masked at any rate; our teeth shouldn't be too discolored or too crooked. Products are created for every manner of defect on our bodies, and sometimes defects are created so that products can be sold or so that we can unreasonably obsess over another imperfect body part that does not live up to cultural expectations.

A few years ago, social media told us that a truly worthy body would have a "thigh gap": that is, a space between the thighs when a woman puts her knees together. Never mind that for many women, a thigh gap is impossible to attain because of the way their hips are built. Besides: the idea of a gap in one's thighs seems completely arbitrary. What about a thigh gap makes legs more beautiful and worthy? And yet teen girls started taking pictures of their legs, seeking the holy grail of a thigh gap, despairing if no gap existed. Grown women, too, have obsessed over their thighs by seeking thigh-specific workouts and finding all kinds of advice online about how to achieve more space between their thighs. Discussions on social media were driven by the hashtag #thighgap, and women posted pictures of thin women as motivation to achieve the thigh gap goal. Plenty of other articles discussed whether men found the thigh gap attractive. This is just one indication that conversations about beauty are driven mostly by the desire to be alluring to others, both men and women, rather than simple satisfaction for the self.

If we needed any evidence that standards of beauty are a cultural construct, the thigh gap trend could be exhibit A. The fifteenth-century artist Botticelli certainly didn't find thin legs attractive; the women he painted had thick, voluptuous thighs. Even now, some non-Western cultures assume women who are stick-thin are unhealthy and unattractive, and that plumpness is a body type to which women should aspire. Yet in the United States and other Western cultures, a plump form is considered revolting, and those who are overweight learn early that their bodies are shameful, a clear mark of their unworthiness. In *Shrill*, author Lindy West articulates the ways a fat body, and in particular a fat woman's body, is treated as an object of scorn.

As a woman, my body is scrutinized, policed, and treated as a public commodity. As a fat woman, my body is also lampooned, openly reviled, and associated with moral and intellectual failure. My body limits my job prospects, access to medical care and fair trials, and—the one thing Hollywood movies and Internet trolls most agree on—my ability to be loved. So the subtext, when a thin person asks a fat person, "Where do you get your confidence?" is, "You must be some sort of alien because if I looked like you, I would definitely throw myself into the sea."[4]

West provides an incisive critique of contemporary culture's ability to determine who should be deemed acceptable solely on the basis of body size. When we talk about our embodied selves, then, the thin ideal becomes a significant part of our discussion, and those who fail to meet that ideal—even if only in their perception—believe that they are not worthy. According to a 2008 survey, 75 percent of women reported unhealthy feelings about their bodies and food.[5] It is no wonder that weight loss in the United States has become a $60 billion a year industry.[6]

EXPECTATIONS ABOUT BODY SIZE are only one of many ways we realize we are not good enough, our bodies not worthy enough. As an adolescent, I learned that my hair wasn't exactly right, nor was my athletic build or my flat chest. Today, some thirty years later, those whose appearance exists outside of gender-normative expectations still face significant levels of bullying, letting them know that they are also unworthy of acceptance and respect. By some measures, those who are transgender or gender nonconforming face substantially higher suicide rates, in great part because they are told their bodies, and thus their selves, are to be reviled.

Those with disabilities are likewise scorned because their bodies do not meet expectations our culture has established—scorned so much, in fact, that many become invisible, people we do not see because their bodies are so far outside what we consider normal. We cannot imagine those with physical disabilities to be fully whole, and sometimes in Christian circles, those with disabilities get prayed over as if the bodies they inhabit somehow demand a healing miracle to be accepted.

Indeed, for all the lip service Christians give to being focused more on our spiritual selves than our physical selves, Christian culture sends muddied messages about standards of beauty and bodily worthiness, establishing expectations that are in practice little different from those of broader culture, while also conveying that we should remain focused primarily on our hearts and minds. That Bibles marketed to girls include makeup and clothing tips designed to help them be appealing suggests that Christian culture is not exactly clear about what expectations it should establish regarding appearance. Plenty of Christian self-help publications for adults also affirm that God values inner beauty . . . while also dishing out advice about diets and clothing and improving one's physical image in order to find a spouse or to keep one's spouse invested in marriage. As I mentioned earlier, several prominent Christian leaders, including Mark Driscoll, Pat Robertson, and Tim Challies, have suggested that women who "let themselves go" physically are at fault when their husbands stray, and that keeping up appearances is one of the tasks women should perform in their marriages. Challies asserts that women "express their love and respect for husbands" through their outer beauty, and brushed hair and an attractive sweater reveal that a woman has inner beauty too.[7]

For many in Christian culture, expectations about the body and beauty standards are wrapped up in notions of femininity. Contemporary movements in presumably "biblical" womanhood make femininity foundational, and women are told that being feminine is a biblical principle. The caveat— that femininity is both an inner and an outer trait—does little to diminish the sense that being feminine is a high calling to which all women should aspire. Christian women learn that being feminine is written into our DNA, part of God's design, and that popular culture has eroded women's sense of femininity. It is because of this "secular" culture that too many women dress and act like men instead of accepting their God-designated femininity.

Women immersed in evangelical culture hear that women who do not embrace their femininity—who do not wear feminine clothes that distinguish their bodies from men's—are capitulating to the lies of popular culture that make women equal to men. In numerous testimonies published online, women suggest they were mired in sin until they discovered their feminine side, and that a rejection of skirts and dresses reflected their rejection of God. "God created women to be beautiful, nurturing, and feminine," one writer insists. "It is ok for you to buck how society expects you to dress and act, and instead do what God MADE you to do. It's ok for you to appear to be feminine, naïve, and innocent, because those are qualities Christ instructed us to have."[8] Bible studies, like Mary Kassain and Nancy DeMoss's *True Women 101*, promise to help women reclaim their femininity. Another writer, sharing her story for *Charisma* magazine, narrates the experience of having God transform her from tomboy to woman, arguing that "the enemy" was responsible for making her a tomboy, for trying to "steal my femininity," and that it was the Lord who "[made] me into a lady."[9]

I cannot read these assertions without thinking back to my childhood and my teen years. This pressure to conform, to make one's appearance more feminine, must also affect other girls like me, girls whose sense of style turns toward basketball shorts and tennis shoes but who must surely hear that "the enemy" is trying to "steal" their femininity. Like my younger self, these girls discover that being themselves means being maligned and misunderstood. Given my own struggle, I cannot imagine the pain and devastation awaiting transgender teens who face intense pressure to live embodied in a gender that does not match their mind or heart. Their culture, Christian or otherwise, likely judges their very existence. Unsurprisingly, by some estimates, nearly 30 percent of transgender teens attempt to take their own lives, and nearly 42 percent report incidences of self-harm, hoping to alter or destroy the bodies they've been taught to revile.[10]

Most of us learn to dislike the bodies we've been given, so perhaps this is merely a difference by degrees. We all hear, from both popular and Christian culture, that our bodies must conform to a certain standard established more by fiat than by fact. Our bodies need to be transformed to be deemed worthy, even if they are fearfully and wonderfully made. And I—and a multitude of others like me—have also heard this: To be a woman means to be feminine. To be feminine means to accept God's design for our lives. To be a tomboy means to be beholden to the enemy.

To be me means to not be enough.

AS A RUNNER, I enjoy nothing more than hitting the roads on a sunny spring morning. Cresting a hill in Newberg allows me to see a valley full of orchards blooming, with mountains in the distance, the sun's warmth not yet unbearable. For years, I've worn shorts, a sports bra, and a tank top on such mornings, and I love the feeling of sun on my bare shoulders.

I never felt sheepish about wearing so little on my runs— never, that is, until a man drove by with a catcall and a whistle, revving his car's engine. At such moments, when a catcall signals expectations about who—or more accurately *what*—I am, I often wonder what compels someone to intentionally make a woman uncomfortable. Although I acknowledge that millions of such men do exist, as attested by the rates of sexual assault and rape worldwide, I still wonder whether whistles and revving engines are intended to unsettle me or titillate me. But no, the man cares nothing for me or the safety in which I hope to exercise. I am only an object for his pleasure, nothing more.

Because this is another expectation we have about our bodies: that despite being perpetually imperfect, our bodies are made to be objects for others' enjoyment. To say that women are "objectified" in such moments seems too strong a statement, especially because objectification has become freighted with countless connotations. Even my kids don't understand what I mean, really, when I rail against them for objectifying others: for talking about the "hot" girl in their classes, or for making comments about some woman they see standing curbside.

Still, at a time when many seem to think that sexism and misogyny are things of the past, a man has ascended to the country's highest office even after he was heard commenting on women's sexuality, seeing them not as real people but as walking sex organs he hoped to grab. Although Donald Trump was widely criticized for these comments, plenty of people excused his behavior as "locker room talk," something that men engage in with each other behind closed doors. As if that made the objectification of women's bodies any better. As if we all expect men to behave this way.

The #MeToo movement that unfolded in the fall of 2017 suggests that for too long, some men in power *have* behaved as badly as President Trump, their misogyny fueling harassment and assault. When the *New York Times* and the *New Yorker* published investigative reports detailing the lecherous behavior of movie mogul Harvey Weinstein, a new movement was born, and women from many walks of life have come forward to tell their stories about the behavior of men—sometimes criminal, sometimes not, but almost always inappropriate. The #MeToo movement has cast a wide net, exposing the nefarious behavior of beloved cultural icons such as Garrison Keillor of *Prairie Home Companion* fame; Charlie Rose, the anchor for *CBS This Morning*; and senator and one-time comedian Al Franken, who resigned from the U.S. Senate as the result of sexual harassment accusations. A #churchtoo Twitter campaign followed #MeToo, with Christians taking to social media to tell their stories of times that church sanctuaries provided no sanctuary at all: not from harassment, nor assault, nor rape.

To many, the magnitude of #MeToo—the many women who report being harassed or assaulted—is not very surprising, because we are continuing to raise young men in a culture that tells them women's bodies are to be used for their own enjoyment, that they are expected to ogle women or to be tantalized by a woman's form. Boys in Western culture are assailed with images of scantily clad women that are used to sell everything from alcohol to video games to sex. According to some estimates, by the age of seventeen, 93 percent of boys have viewed pornography.[11] Even the best parental firewalls cannot keep boys from seeing and objectifying women's bodies again and again, especially when peers at school can provide the screens for such viewing. But it's not just pornography. Video games sexualize women's bodies while also conveying a sense of hypermasculinity that glorifies violence, sometimes against women. The same hypermasculinity, so pervasive in all corners of our culture, tells young men that their bodies need to be strong and overpowering, and those boys and men who cannot exude strength are told to stop being "girlie" or "feminine." One of my son's coaches castigated boys by yelling at them to "stop being [a pejorative word for female genitalia]," using women's bodies as an insult and an embarrassment. In the documentary *The Masks We Wear*, several experts note the persistent messages boys receive: to be feminine is to be despised, and the female form is fundamentally for men's pleasure. Given these confusing and sometimes contradictory messages about women, it's not hard to see why so many young women and men have unhealthy relationships with bodies: their own and those of others.

Concurrent to the messages they hear about women's bodies and men's authority over them, women are also told that they can find great power in the ability to enchant and coerce men by their bodies alone. This notion is at times presented as a positive attribute, and some feminists see sexuality as a form of women's empowerment, an opportunity for women to claim agency over their bodies, to decide how, and with whom, they will use their bodies. Believing that for millennia men have had complete power over women, often to violent ends, this form of feminist expression argues that women must reclaim their power and that the autonomy of their bodies is part of their reclamation.

But in Christian culture especially, women are reminded that their powerful sexuality is a detriment and that they bear responsibility when men stumble, lusting in their hearts and minds or capitulating to sex outside of heterosexual marriage. The corollary message about men is that they have no defenses against their basest desires. Messages about modesty and purity are legion in Christian culture, and are based on the notion that women must sublimate their sexuality because of its vast power.

Accordingly, those women who have sex before marriage are seen as unredeemable damaged goods. Youth group activities sometimes drive home this point with object lessons: a much-handled twenty-dollar bill, a chewed-up piece of gum, a rose that's been plucked of its petals. Whatever the intent of these lessons, the shame that must result from such messages about sex and sexuality is certain. On the one hand, girls hear that their bodies are powerful, amazing, alluring—but only if they keep themselves pure. Once they've "fallen," their bodies no longer amazing, they will be unloved and unworthy, out of reach of everyone's grace, except for God's.

An entire marketing apparatus has been developed to remind Christian girls and women that their body's purity is sacrosanct. There are purity balls, at which dads can pledge to uphold and protect their daughter's virginity until appropriate suitors arrive to court and marry them. The purity balls are much like proms, with elaborate decorations and girls in fancy white dresses— except at these balls, dads dance with their daughters and a commitment ceremony makes space for fathers to promise fidelity to daughters who vow to keep their bodies pure. No corollary events exist for mothers and sons—but then again, boys are not beholden to the same rules of purity, their bodies being more likely to be tempted than to tempt. There are purity rings, some of them quite costly, which a father can give to his daughter to wear on her ring finger as a concrete reminder that she is to remain sexually pure and that her father is to guard this purity until her wedding day, when a suitor can offer her a different ring. T-shirts announcing girls' purity are also mass-marketed to Christians, with slogans reminding others that there is "No trespassing" on the wearer's body, because her "father is watching." "Modest is hottest" T-shirts, the words emblazoned across a woman's chest, both sexualize women's bodies, letting others know they are "hot," and sublimate sexuality with suggestions of modesty. Such products are rarely made for boys and men, whose purity is apparently less precious, less required.

Given the extraordinary power of women's bodies and the expectation of sexual purity, Christian women are taught to hide their female form while also retaining a sense of the feminine. Women in religious traditions like the Amish understand this practice well, and their long dresses, with long sleeves and cape aprons, serve the significant function of keeping their bodies hidden. Other conservative Christian traditions are not as extreme, although women are still expected to cover their shoulders and legs, and girls are taught from an early age specific rules for modesty: that a tank top strap must be at least three fingers wide, that shorts must brush the knee, that if the belly shows when a girl stretches her arms over her head, the shirt is too immodest. These rules, too, have become marketable, and websites like Secret Keeper Girl provide guidance for how girls can keep their best, most secret gift (that is, their body) hidden until marriage.

Every spring, my university campus hosts a large conference for conservative Christian homeschool families. I realize the conference is under way when hundreds of people descend on the quad, the women and girls in long dresses, the men and boys in slacks and collared shirts. On the last day, the kids, mostly teenagers, take to the track for athletic competition. And while the boys run races with shorts and T-shirts, the girls compete in dresses that fall below the knees. I'm struck every year by the double standard. The boys run unfettered, their legs swift and unencumbered. The girls, meanwhile, are dragged down by the skirts they wear, the fabric tangling around their knees, making it difficult to feel the freedom running can offer.

My office, which looks out over the track, gives me a perfect perch from which to watch these teens circle the track. The homeschool track meet serves for me as an important metaphor for the ways Christian culture shapes—and distorts—the relationships we have to our embodied selves, and the ways messages about modesty and bodily shame can encumber us and keep us from being free to celebrate the amazing bodies God has created, in all their wonder, strength, and diversity. I wonder how much faster the girls might run if not for the fetters of cloth and expectation.

AT THE 2015 LONDON MARATHON, Kiran Gandhi decided to race while she had her period. This is in itself not unusual, since countless female athletes compete during their menstrual cycles. But Gandhi made an intentional choice to let her blood run freely during the race, rather than using hygiene products, to call attention to the many women worldwide who lack access to feminine products.

Her critics called Gandhi "disgusting" and "unladylike." I must admit to being unsettled by her decision as well, wondering if her free-bleeding marathon was really necessary to make a point about women's bodies, or whether it was merely a publicity stunt. Fundamentally, though, Gandhi's marathon reminds us how uncomfortable many of us are with the natural processes that occur with women's bodies, and how shrouded in shame these processes can be. Even though almost every woman on the planet has a monthly period at some point during her life, we tend to act as if periods don't exist, relying on all manner of products to hide the truth: pocket-size tampons we can covertly take to bathrooms; tapered pads that can be worn beneath tight pants; and lotions, perfumes, powders, and douches to mask any potentially unpleasant smell that might call attention to a woman's scent.

In some cultures, this shame about a woman's body is put on steroids, so to speak. During their periods, women without access to feminine products may be unable to leave home for school or work. As such, lack of access to feminine products becomes one of many ways women are kept uneducated and powerless. For most women in the United States, access to these products isn't the problem; the problem is the unfounded belief that women on their periods are hormonal beasts, incapable of rational thought and thus unproductive in the workplace. A strong woman with vocal opinions is sometimes seen as being "on the rag," irrational because of raging hormones. Comedic movies play on these stereotypes, and though we might laugh, the mythology of an out-of-control woman on her period drives our perceptions about menstruation, PMS, and women's ability to be calm or hysterical, given that time of the month.

Like most girls, I received mixed messages about my period. According to Judy Blume's *Are You There God? It's Me, Margaret*, the handbook for every girl I knew who was reaching puberty, having a period was something to anticipate with wonder, but also something to fear. Advertisers compounded the sense that I should dread getting my period, that it would knock me out cold with cramps and flummox me with awkward situations. The commercials also promised freedom, if only I purchased what they were selling. Given my already intense discomfort with my female body, the horror of a period intensified these messages, and I spent years longing for menopause, to be done with this monthly shame. I also longed to be as unburdened as the women I saw in commercials, running freely through fields of daisies in their white pants. But what I experienced—and what my friends experienced, when they admitted as much—was far more shameful. We were all embarrassed, to some degree, and for at least a few days each month, we hated the female bodies we'd been given.

But the menstrual cycle is not the only natural process that women are told should make them feel shame. Recent cultural conversations about women nursing in public also remind us of the tension that exists everywhere in Western culture. On the one hand, women's breasts are sexualized in our culture, and marketers use images of women's breasts to sell everything from beer to clothing to hamburgers. When treated as objects to be desired, to titillate, to ogle and caress, visual images of breasts are acceptable, and we assume as completely normal those women wearing bikinis beachside, their barely covered breasts visible for all to see. But women nursing in public—even with their breasts completely out of sight—have been asked to retreat to bathroom stalls to breastfeed and have been bullied into leaving restaurants or shopping malls or even swimming pools where women in bikinis are legion. This seeming double standard only reinforces the notion that women's bodies are best seen as objects, intended for the pleasure, visual or otherwise, of men. When women's bodies are used to provide sustenance to children, they become disgusting, just one more way the female form is reviled.

Kiran Gandhi, writing about her marathon experience, noted that "culture is happy to speak about and objectify the parts of the body that can be sexually consumed by others. . . . But the moment we talk about something that is not for the enjoyment of others, like a period, everyone becomes deeply uncomfortable."[12] Attempts to make women cover up when breastfeeding (or to breastfeed in private spaces, like bathroom stalls) shows how confused our cultural messages about women's bodies can be.

Even though I've never been pregnant or given birth, I find the labor metaphors in the Bible intriguing, perhaps because they challenge the shame we often feel about women's bodies. Isaiah 42:14 describes God as a mother in labor, gasping and panting as she gives birth; in a subsequent chapter, Isaiah compares God to a nursing mother. In John 3, Jesus relies on a birthing metaphor to relate the ways we can be born again by following him. Because of our overwhelming reliance on masculine language when talking about God, we often overlook this figurative language and its power to change the way we understand and accept the sacredness of our bodies. If we understood our embodied selves as vessels of the living God, as image-bearers of our Creator, reflecting the incarnation, I imagine we might work harder to accept, without shame, the bodies we've been given.

WHEN I WAS YOUNG and accompanied my grandma to her hair appointments, the older women in the salon would fawn over me and my blond curls, telling me they paid good money to make their hair do what mine did naturally. I could never understand this fascination with my hair, and I've sometimes said, only half joking, that my life would have been far different if not for my naturally curly hair.

If I could have had long straight hair as a child, perhaps people wouldn't have mistaken me for a boy. If I could have feathered my hair as a teen, perhaps boys would have liked me more. If I could have had big, beautiful bangs in college, perhaps I'd have had more dates, and wouldn't have spent my twenties desperately seeking The One. This imagining all sounds so superficial, so trivial, but given how appearance-driven our culture is, I know there is some truth to my wonderings. Hair does make a girl, after all.

But maybe it's not my hair that needed to be changed but the way other people saw and judged me. Let's face it: we judge people all the time when their bodies don't fit into our paradigm of what is normal, of what we deem acceptable. Recent battles about whether transgender people should use public restrooms appropriate to their gender identity or to the sex listed on their birth certificates reflect this sense of deep discomfort with those whose bodies don't fit the categories we've created. Despite claims that requiring people to use restrooms that match the sex on their birth certificate is about children's safety and keeping predators away from kids, the truth is that people tend to revile those who live in bodies they don't understand. Often that means reviling our own bodies, too, in all the inexplicable intricacy of our physical forms, in all the ways we fail to live up to what others say is expected of our embodied selves.

This inexplicable intricacy matters—or it should, if only we were free to accept our bodies as fearfully, wonderfully made, no matter what they look like. But no; we are much more likely to recognize what is wrong with our bodies than everything that is right. Too many of us obsess over the blemishes on our skin when we should be marveling at the awesome function of the human body's largest organ. We perseverate over weight gained and lost when we might do better to recognize the body's ability to adapt, acknowledging the ways people have survived in challenging times, the resilience of our human forms, and the ability to keep going even when fuel isn't in the offing. Whatever shape our bodies take, we need to remember that we are all a living, breathing testament to the nature of our Creator, who designed a vastly complicated body system and then called it good.

Finding yourself in a world expecting someone else means finding your body acceptable too. This work is difficult, for sure, and I am just now starting to celebrate the beautiful female form I've walked in for almost fifty years. (Even saying my female form is "beautiful" is difficult, because I've heard for too long that this is not the case.) For me, this work of embracing my body has required pushing back against all those messages telling me I needed to buy just one more product to make my hair less curly. Or that possessing a female body comes with certain responsibilities: to wear makeup and high heels, when I preferred tennis shoes and cutoffs; to be always perfectly groomed for my partner, letting him decide what counted as attractive. It's meant accepting my sensuality, even when doing so goes against everything I've been told about female sexuality and power.

I want so badly for my kids to know a different world, one in which their unique bodies can be celebrated rather than reviled. I've tried to alter the way I talk about my body, hoping to redirect some of the shame I experienced growing up, hoping that they will find themselves worthy in the bodies God created for them. But they already recognize ways in which their embodied selves are considered less-than, because their skin pigment is darker and their stature is different than many of their peers. My younger son has been graced with curly hair, which has been a constant frustration for him, as it once was for me. He desperately wants to have hair similar to what he sees on screen, where straight hair and luscious bangs are a thing, for boys as well as girls. Hair makes a boy sometimes too.

Popular culture is starting to shift narratives about our bodies, though, so I haven't given up hope completely that we will all be stuck, navigating bodies we despise. Stars like Lena Dunham and Melissa McCarthy affirm that beautiful bodies come in many shapes, and roles once reserved only for nimble starlets are now going to women with different shapes entirely. Other figures, including Beyoncé and Lady Gaga, have spoken publicly about body acceptance, and theirs is a message that has been picked up by women like Amanda Martinez Beck and J. Nicole Morgan, whose new *Fat and Faithful* podcast aims to address body acceptance in the context of Christianity. Roxane Gay's astounding 2017 memoir, *Hunger*, pushes against every assumption people hold about those who are fat, and argues convincingly that a culture that regularly shames bodies has lost its center.

If that center has been lost, it certainly can be found, in the ways we talk about each other's embodied selves, in the ways we talk about our own. I'm grateful that some young people today are starting to hear different messages in their churches, even, about sex and sexuality, because those messages translate to a different understanding of bodily shame. Mainstream evangelical publications like *Christianity Today* are challenging the "modest is hottest" ideology, rightfully naming the ways an overfocus on modesty and purity often uses shaming language to objectify women. Writing for *Christianity Today*, Sharon Hodde Miller affirms that the church needs to reframe how it talks about our embodied forms, affirming that women's bodies are not inherently tempting, something to be hidden away because they cause others to stumble; instead, she writes, "women's bodies glorify God," a belief that should change the way Christians think about women's forms—and about men's as well.[13]

Recent research suggests there is a strong link between many Christians' views about the body and the theological understanding of what it means to be "fearfully, wonderfully made." One study, reported in the *Journal of Religion and Health*, found that Christians who viewed their bodies as sinful and separated from their souls were more likely to report bodily shame than those who believed in a more holistic understanding of the self, in which the body and the soul are both sacred. According to the survey, "beliefs reflecting Christian teachings that one's body is a temple of God, created specifically by God, and that God is glorified and honored through one's body, were linked to appreciating one's body."[14]

Too often in my life, I've heard "Your body is a temple" as a different kind of shaming mechanism. You know, *stop eating so much sugar*, or *don't drink so much Diet Coke*, because your body is a temple and should not be defiled. But perhaps it's time to reclaim an understanding of the body as a temple that is holy and sacred, no matter its form. We need to intentionally celebrate our bodies as one more way we reflect our Creator, in all the beautiful, diverse—and beautifully diverse—ways our bodies are created.

Believing that we are fearfully and wonderfully made would mean embracing the radical belief that our bodies are perfect, even in their seeming imperfections. When we see messages everywhere telling us what presumably perfect bodies should look like, we can remember that these messages are manufactured, that they have no basis in reality, that they are as deceptive as the photoshopped models on magazine covers, tempting us to feel less worthy because we lack a thigh gap, or a golden tan, or even straight, feathered hair, for that matter. If we want to find ourselves in a different kind of world, we need the courage to accept our own bodies and those of others, too, who are beautiful just as they are.

Someday, and perhaps even someday soon, I will find myself in this kind of world. And when I do, I will take my curly hair, my stiff hips, my decidedly uncool sway, and I will dance. Because my body, in all its intricacy, is worthy of that kind of celebration.

8

WHAT'S THE MATTER WITH BEING BLESSED

Just days after returning from Vietnam with our seven-month-old son, whom we had adopted from a suburb of Ho Chi Minh City, I walked across campus, feeling very maternal and very tired. Benjamin Quan was strapped to my chest in a BabyBjörn, facing outward, both because he loved to see the world and because of his tendency to projectile vomit. With Benjamin in the baby carrier, I could lean my head forward and rub my chin over the wisps of his hair, which I did often as we walked. His tiny head was a tangible reminder of the seeming miracle that had occurred: this child, born far too early and thousands of miles away, had made me the luckiest mother in the world.

On my jaunt across campus, several folks stopped me to meet Benjamin and to hear about the experiences that Ron and I had when we went to Vietnam to bring him home. As has happened often—especially when my sons were both young and incredibly precious-looking—someone remarked that Benjamin was so blessed to have been adopted. It was so amazing, they said, that God had made the universe move in such a way that Ben could land in our family rather than remain in the orphanage or in Vietnam, where his upbringing might have been far more impoverished.

Back then, as a new mother, I didn't know quite what to say to such comments. It *had* felt like the universe, or God, had conspired to bring Benjamin to us. But something didn't feel exactly right about the idea that Benjamin was blessed to be with us. After all, I'd only been a mother for two weeks by that point, and it wasn't even clear how good I might be at this parenting gig.

Over time, and with the subsequent adoption of our second son, I began to understand better why I saw such comments as problematic. If God had intervened to make sure I was Benjamin's mother, then God had a problem. And if Benjamin was *blessed* to be in our family, rather than any other, then the idea of blessing was completely messed up. Because for Benjamin to receive this blessing, he had to first experience a devastating loss: of his birth mother, of his birth family, of his culture and history. Furthermore, if God had engineered the world so we could have Benjamin Quan, that could mean that another woman somewhere in Bien Hoa had experienced her own significant loss. I couldn't imagine a God who would make a woman in a developing country suffer just so a woman of power and privilege could swoop in and raise her child. How could my overwhelming joy—first for Benjamin and then for Samuel Saurabh, adopted three years later when he was three—result from the sorrow of other women? The Christian language of blessing, and the worldview it represented, seemed wholly incapable of answering these questions.

Yet many of us, raised in Christian culture and shaped by its language and narratives, feel that we should be able to see God's hand in all that happens, both the good and the bad. Families who experience tragedies are told that God allows things to happen for some greater purpose, or that God is refining them by making them walk through life's trials. When something good happens, Christians often proclaim that they have been blessed by God, or that God has coordinated circumstances so that goodness is the end result. People in my neck of the woods often talk about a fortuitous event as a "God thing": for example, adopting a child like Benjamin instead of another baby was totally a God thing, because Benjamin fits so well into our family.

Rarely do Christians question the ways this theology establishes expectations about how we talk about human suffering and loss. If we find ourselves in a world with a capricious God, our entire understanding of ourselves and our universe shifts: those who meet good fortune do so because they are worthy of God's favor, and those who meet tragedy and disaster must have done something wrong, because God has chosen to punish or shape or teach them. Some people are inclined to use this worldview as a bludgeon, suggesting that God will rain terror down on those who sin while providing the faithful with material abundance. But sometimes good things happen to the undeserving, and suffering comes to those who are righteous. Our language, our theology, and our perspective need to reflect this reality. Otherwise, some people will believe themselves unworthy of God's unconditional love, grace, and mercy—a mercy that reaches the just and the unjust alike.

SEVERAL YEARS AGO, I was part of a committee that had interminably long meetings. Actually, any committee meeting can seem interminably long to me. But being part of this particular committee was its own kind of punishment, especially because the chair was scattered and chatty and self-important, which meant that conversations got derailed by minutiae, name-dropping, and protracted stories about presumably well-connected people the committee chair knew. One evening, during a meeting that went hours past its announced ending point and hours past my bedtime, I sat at our committee table at a low boil, stewing about the wasted time I was spending listening to the chair prattle on about her own awesomeness.

The next day, on social media, the chair posted a photo of the meeting, my tension and anger especially obvious alongside the chair's excitement. My chin and neck were visibly strained by stress, while the chair, sitting next to me, smiled brightly. The photo's caption? "The committee was a blessing, we were blessed, the meeting was blessèd: #blessed, everywhere." My low boil returned, because I could not believe she could see anything that had happened in our meeting as a blessing.

Working on that committee—and seeing the chair's social media post—became a tipping point for me. It was as if the scales had been removed from my eyes and I could see so clearly how using the word *blessed* can shape our sense of reality. By asserting that a meeting where some people were obviously miserable was "blessed," the chair had shifted public perceptions about our work. Her words obfuscated her role in making that meeting—and the event we were planning—a frustrating experience. At that moment, I finally saw how problematic the language of blessing can be, and I decided to stop using the word altogether.

This may seem like an extraordinarily cynical decision, especially because the Bible uses the language of blessing often. Scripture contains countless passages that address the idea of blessing: the psalmist reminds us that blessings fall to those who keep God's precepts (Psalm 119:56) and that God bestows blessings on those who follow God (Psalm 21:6); the Sermon on the Mount offers a long list of those who are blessed. Our worship songs acknowledge that God blesses our souls, that those who worship God will be blessed, that we are supposed to bless the Lord (although this assertion of blessing God has always perplexed me). And while I would argue that all of us are blessed because we are formed in God's image, too often the language of blessing has been used to establish expectations for how we walk through the world. It has marginalized and alienated those who might not receive God's blessing in the ways we've conceived of it. Too often, the language of blessing has created division, affirming that some people are more worthy of God's blessing than others.

Proponents of a prosperity gospel tell followers that God provides monetary reward and good health to those who are faithful, and thus have distorted the idea of blessing. Pastors like Joel Osteen and Benny Hinn created their substantial empires by promising that God wants believers to be wealthy, and that those Christians with loads of money deserve what they've been given. Osteen asserts that we only need believe it to achieve it, and that material wealth results when we faithfully assume God will bless us. "To experience [God's] immeasurable favor, you must rid yourself of that small-minded thinking and start expecting God's blessings, start anticipating promotion and supernatural increase," writes Osteen. "You must conceive it in your heart before you can receive it. In other words, you must make increase in your own thinking, then God will bring those things to pass."[1] In Osteen's world, those who remain poor have only themselves and their lack of faith to blame. The faithful will, in good time, have whatever their hearts desire.

Despite biblical evidence to the contrary, despite all the Bible verses suggesting a far different vision for the wealthy, the prosperity gospel also maintains that material goods are a clear marker of God's blessing. Nothing says "Jesus loves me" like a three-car garage and a Lexus. For some Christians, this has meant pursuing the good life at significant cost, the hope of acquiring earthly possessions to show God's blessing instead causing financial ruin. Writing for the *Washington Post*, Cathleen Falsani notes, "The gospel of prosperity turns Christianity into a vapid bless-me club, with a doctrine that amounts to little more than spiritual magical thinking: If you pray the right way, God will make you rich."[2] The language of blessing, in this instance, reflects one's worthiness, leading those who are poor, or ill, or downtrodden to believe that their suffering means they are outside God's love.

It might be easy to accept that Jesus' gospel and the prosperity gospel are discordant, and that wealth and physical well-being have little to do with one's faithfulness or with God's blessing. Yet many people persist in talking about being "blessed" by God in ways that suggest a connection between one's worthiness and God's favor. The "ring by spring" culture I experienced at the evangelical college I attended was one example of this. As an undergrad, I heard over and over again that my friends had been "blessed" by finding The One. Similarly, when folks say they have been blessed by God for each child they've conceived, carried, and delivered, I am reminded of those who have struggled mightily with fertility and will never know this kind of blessing. Of those who may have conceived and miscarried. Of those who may have delivered children who, because of some trauma in the womb or at birth that requires long-term care, have turned their lives upside down. Will we say—or more pointedly, will we truly believe—that God also blesses these parents?

What does it really mean to say we have received God's blessing?

A number of writers have, in recent years, critiqued the idea of being "blessed," calling attention to the ways that language establishes expectations for how we understand God, good fortune, and our relationships to each other. In the *New York Times*, Jessica Bennett explores the ways the social media hashtag #blessed has become a cultural shorthand for being lucky, or a way to boast about one's amazing life. "There's nothing quite like invoking holiness as a way to brag about your life," writes Bennett. "But calling something 'blessed' has become the go-to term for those who want to boast about an accomplishment while pretending to be humble, fish for a compliment, acknowledge a success (without sounding too conceited), or purposely elicit envy."[3]

A casual glance through Twitter on one spring day shows football players being #blessed by the NFL draft; a few teenage girls #blessed by spring break and a few others #blessed to be asked to prom; and someone #blessed because his social media followers now exceed 100k. While I wonder how the football players who didn't get an NFL pick must feel, and whether those girls who weren't asked to prom also recognize God's blessing, I also wonder about the children in Syria who were killed today when a U.S.-led coalition bombed their school. If we follow the language of God's blessing to its logical conclusion, we might also be suggesting that kids born in Syria are somehow less worthy than a girl in Texas who went on spring break with her bestie.

When I read about news items like that bombing, I feel unsettled by my own dumb luck of having been born in Illinois and not Syria. Because of this, I don't have to worry that when I send my kids to school they could be murdered by air raids. Sometimes it hits me how much of the richness in my life is based not on anything I've done or not done. God has not rewarded me for saying no to drugs, avoiding extramarital sex, and attending church most every Sunday of my life. I was fortunate to be the daughter of two middle-class, educated white people living in a prosperous country. My life has been relatively unmarred by illness, and my body has been strong and healthy. By some good fortune, I get to be a mom to two incredible teenage kids, stepmom to two great adults, and now grandmother to two healthy boys.

To say I am "blessed" by all this suggests that God is some kind of impetuous gift-giver, deciding who receives goodness and who does not. To say I am blessed conveys the sense that what I've done makes me more deserving of God's abundance—that we live in a divine meritocracy of sorts, in which the hardworking folks receive extra earthly rewards. So I avoid the word, freighted with expectation. Instead, I admit that I am grateful for these gifts, aware that my good fortune has not been shared by others whose unlucky circumstances—even at their births—means that bombs might rain down on their kids. Jesus' Sermon on the Mount turns our eyes to them, these ones who are blessed, for they truly will be part of God's world.

IN 2012, Jessica Kelley's son, Henry, was diagnosed with an aggressive brain tumor that ultimately killed him. He was four years old, and the last months of his life were tortured, his illness and the pain of an ever-growing mass changing a bright, active child into one who endured searing headaches, a loss of mobility and language, and an awful death. Kelley narrates Henry's life and death in her beautiful book, *Lord Willing?*, which also considers the ways far too many Christians grapple with suffering: by accepting what Kelley calls a blueprint theology, which explains suffering by acknowledging "God's great plan" for every aspect of our lives. According to blueprint theology, everything happens for a reason, and even horrible tragedies have some larger meaning.

Kelley's experience of losing her son caused her to challenge this perspective and the language used to grapple with pain and suffering. In the aftermath of her son's death, Kelley heard often from others that God had a plan for Henry, a plan that included his death. She was given books by Christian writers who explain the blueprint theology, writing out of their own pain and suggesting that God causes tragedies to draw people closer to God; or that God causes tragedies to teach us lessons; or that God causes tragedies because God's plan is bigger, more mysterious, more amazing than anything we can fathom.

Although such language about God's place in suffering is meant to provide comfort, it also establishes expectations for how we are to see and understand God, as well as the often chaotic, inexplicable world in which we live. Kelley argues convincingly that the blueprint theology—the idea that everything happens according to God's plan—requires an unsettling understanding of God. Either God *causes* everything to happen for a reason, and is therefore vindictive and heedless of the pain people incur for some purpose only God knows, or God *allows* everything to happen for some mysterious greater good, standing aside while people suffer as a way of inexplicably glorifying God's power.

Messages about God's specific plan for our lives, especially in the midst of suffering, are legion. The shelves in Christian bookstores bend beneath the weight of books promising to explain God's plan and to help readers figure out what God wants for them, often in three easy steps. Such books assert that God's sovereignty means that God knows all about what we will do, and opens and closes doors for us to walk through, if only we trust God. In such a view, doors that slam in our face, causing great pain, are God's way of redirecting us to the plan God has established. Other books, blogs, and magazine articles explain that God's plan can be fulfilled once someone has accepted Jesus into her heart, and that—according to one writer—"once you have received God's forgiveness . . . you are ready to fulfill the rest of His plan for your life. Your destiny will unfold."[4] In this "God has a plan" ideology, the Big Jesus Moment of conversion unlocks a secret door to your life's blueprint. Christian sympathy cards remind us that the death of a loved one is part of God's bigger plan and that we must trust in God despite our heartbreak, a sentiment which seems to diminish the loss we experience.

Kelley's *Lord Willing?* unpacks these explanations of suffering, which are so deeply embedded in Christian culture, and says that such views provide no hope for those who have suffered deeply. Nor do they explain in any way why some divine plan would mean Kelley's child had to die. She wonders why a God of love would allow a child to suffer a painful death for some imagined "great plan." Why would God use this plan to somehow bring glory to God? (And would anyone want to worship a God who caused a child to suffer as a means of reflecting God's own glory?) Why would God use this "plan" as a means of disciplining and refining God's children? Did a four-year-old really need to experience suffering so that others could know God better?

By deconstructing the idea of "God's clear plan" for our lives, Kelley offers a far more redemptive view of God as one whose "very nature and character is love"[5] and who would not choose to permit suffering, either by causing pain or by allowing pain. Through her study of Scripture, Kelley develops the framework for her new understanding of God, a view she carefully lays out in *Lord Willing?* Because of God's unending love for the world God created, Kelley writes, there is free will, and this necessarily means suffering will occur. Jesus' death on the cross shows that God knows and feels suffering but does not cause it. The resurrection reveals that pain will someday be overcome with good, and until that time, God works and weeps alongside those who suffer, a holy partnership bringing good into the world.

And as I was reminded in a sermon series by Gregg Koskela, who was then pastor at Newberg Friends Church in Oregon, God promises to walk with us even through darkness, especially through darkness. Often, God meets us through the love, comfort, and presence of others, holding space with us through suffering. Preaching one week after an eleven-year-old boy in his congregation drowned, Koskela provided a counter-narrative to those who would say this death happened for a reason, as if this could provide solace to a grieving family. As long as the expectation is that we are to accept suffering as God's will, Koskela suggested, we do not fully understand the character of God, who mourns alongside those who mourn. To suggest otherwise means telling those who mourn that God is not fully with them in their suffering, or that God wants them to be someone they cannot be and is using tragedy as a refining tool.

ONE OF MY CLOSE FRIENDS DIED of colon cancer about ten years ago. She was fifty-three years old, a mother of two young adults, and a gifted teacher. During my early years as a professor, as I tried to balance being a new mother with a full-time job, Colleen was a confidante and a mentor. Her office, right across from mine, was a sanctuary of sorts for me, complete with Rolo candy and calm lighting. I fondly remember the many times Colleen talked me down from certain despair, her own experiences as a working mother providing me the wisdom I needed just when I needed it. I was devastated when she told her circle of friends that she'd been diagnosed with stage IV colon cancer, and I prayed often through the next two years as she underwent surgery, chemo, and experimental therapies. She needed to live for her daughters' sake; she had just finished her PhD, and needed to see the fruits of her efforts. I prayed that God would heal her. That God would extend her life. That God would give her more time with her family.

She died anyway. Sooner than most of us had anticipated.

I suppose I could have been angry at God for not healing Colleen. Fortunately, however, my faith had moved beyond the point where a miracle needed to cure Colleen or else my entire faith would be shattered. I still wondered why Colleen died at such a young age, especially when I heard testimonies in church and on Christian radio about the people God *had* healed. But my faith didn't falter . . . not much, at least.

Several years later I experienced another kind of loss, one so painful I spent long days crying by myself, unable to identify God's plan in what happened. My sister, who was my best friend and my mothering comrade and my running partner, had made the decision to move away from Oregon and back to St. Louis after having lived nine years in the Newberg area. Those years of my sons' early childhood had been bearable for me because my sister was nearby, providing me parenting wisdom and encouragement, often when I needed it most. I had visions of raising our kids together, of cousins becoming tight friends into adulthood, of my sister and me growing old side-by-side in matching velour track suits. But those dreams ended when Amy announced that her family was moving, that she needed the community she'd had in St. Louis but couldn't find here. I prayed that she would change her mind. That some force would keep her from moving. That she wouldn't leave me alone to care for our aging parents. That God would see the wisdom of a different plan.

Her family left anyway, devastating me and my kids. And once again, I had to ask God why others got to live happily beside their sisters, well into old age. I'd had long bouts of loneliness in my life, and now, in a few short years, two close friends were no longer in my day-to-day life, making me lonely again. What was the use of prayer, anyway, when even a simple request—like wanting my sister to find joy here, in Newberg—could not be fulfilled? For months after Amy and her family moved, prayers were like dust in my mouth, choking me in anger: anger at my sister for leaving me, anger at God, who didn't seem interested in responding to my request to keep my friends near. First Colleen, and then Amy. What was God up to, anyway?

I IMAGINE I AM NOT ALONE in wondering why God can't answer even our simplest prayers, and whether there is something wrong with us when prayers go unanswered. Those of us who identify as Christian often receive a persistent message about prayers and miracles: those who pray fervently and don't have those prayers answered the way they hope can express dismay or sadness, but must always assume—given cultural teachings about prayer—that a miracle was not in the offing, or that we couldn't see the miracle God clearly delivered. Our ways are not God's ways, and all that. This is evidenced in movies like *Miracles from Heaven*, a 2016 film that tells the story of a sick child whose loved ones pray with fear and trembling. After some magical hocus-pocus, God, amazingly, heals her. And her fractured family is drawn together by her illness, her subsequent fall from a tree, and her remarkable healing.

A rash of other miracle-related films and books solidify the message that if we just pray hard enough, something amazing will happen. If something amazing does *not* materialize, it's surely because we lack faith: in God and God's abilities, or in the power of prayer itself. *Heaven Is for Real*, a film about a toddler who dies, meets Jesus, and is prayed back to life, uses the trope of miraculous prayer to examine the afterlife. Based on a memoir by the boy's father, the film turns on Colton Burpo's illness and miraculous healing and the ways his interaction with Jesus in heaven causes other, different miracles to occur on earth. In 2015, it was revealed that the event at the center of a similar book, *The Boy Who Came Back from Heaven*, was manufactured by the author, a young boy who apparently constructed his elaborate tale for attention. This admission stoked the cynicism of people like me, who see such stories as just another way for marketers to cash in on Christianity and on our collective desire to believe miracles can happen. Oh me of little faith.

If I'm honest, the language Christian culture uses about prayer can be confounding, and it establishes expectations about our worldviews and how we see and relate to God. I've heard people say to pray for all things, even when what I desire is quotidian. I wonder if I truly am too cynical to see God's hand in minutiae.

Despite my frustration with the way Christian language creates expectations about prayer and God's intervention, I still tell people who are struggling that I will be praying for them. At times, the words "I will be praying for you" stick in my throat, too cloying to speak; at times, the phrase seems like a placeholder of sorts, or maybe shorthand for what I really mean, which is "I am thinking of you." Quakers might say "I will hold you in the light," which comes closer to what I want to express, perhaps because the phrase establishes fewer expectations, comes with less weight. It also doesn't readily require that a miracle happen instantaneously. Holding someone in God's light offers the promise of God's presence and comfort. This really is all I have to offer, and all God promises us: that we are indeed worthy of God's presence and comfort, no matter who we are, no matter how or what we pray.

WE FIND OURSELVES in a world where there is immense suffering and pain. Some days, the suffering seems overwhelming: news of another mass shooting, inexplicably taking the lives of people enjoying a concert; or of a natural disaster, leaving millions homeless; or of a famine so severe that babies die in their mothers' arms for want of nourishment. When we find ourselves in this kind of world, we don't know what to do, and we look for reasons to explain away the suffering of others. God's greater plan seems like a good enough reason, a hopeful justification to what feels like overwhelming darkness.

In such a world, we might also look for reasons why some suffer more than others, and may decide that those of us who suffer less are somehow more worthy of God's blessings.

But listen: because of God's unending love for the world God created, there is free will, and this necessarily means suffering will also occur. Jesus' death on the cross shows that God knows and feels suffering, but does not cause it; the resurrection symbolizes that pain will someday be overcome with good. Until that time, God works and weeps alongside those who suffer, a holy partnership bringing good in a world that desperately needs it. To contend with suffering on earth means to mourn with others, providing comfort and seeking to redeem whatever can be redeemed amid loss and heartache.

This theological understanding can feel unsettling, because it means that the bad things that happen in the world may have no explanation. We want so badly to believe that evil people will have their comeuppance and that those who make good choices, stay faithful to God, and attend church most Sundays will be immune to the vagaries of life. We might resist this notion. We might insist that we are, all seven billion of us, created in God's image and loved by God. And still, our actions reflect a different worldview. One need only look at this ideology as it plays out on social media when tragic violence occurs in Western countries and countless people express their "thoughts and prayers" for the victims. When such tragedy strikes places like Syria or Iraq or other developing countries, few "thoughts and prayers" are forthcoming. Even if we are all

loved by God, some people's despair is more worthy of attention and our prayers.

People who tell my sons they are blessed to be adopted
betray a similar sensibility, one that says I will be a better parent to them merely by virtue of my privilege and the material
goods I can offer them, and that I am more worthy of having
Benjamin Quan and Samuel Saurabh in my life than their first
mothers were. This is categorically untrue. God's plan was not
for other women to carry these babies and then give them up to
an orphanage so I could raise them. Nor was it God's plan that
these women experience the kind of difficulties in their lives
that necessitated my sons' relinquishment. Although we don't
know the specific reasons my sons were left in an orphanage as
infants, we know the general circumstances in their countries
of origin that made it difficult for their mothers to raise them:
poverty, illness, the stigma of being an unwed mother. None
of these circumstances warrant the loss and consequent suffering women must feel when they relinquish their children to
be raised by someone else. I did nothing to merit the great joy
I've experienced in being Ben's mom and Sam's mom. We are
all worthy of God's love, even when a theology which demands
that God's plan engineered all of this would argue otherwise.

Early in my marriage to Ron, and knee-deep in my acceptance of a blueprint theology, it was hard for me to understand why God would have allowed Ron's first marriage to
crumble so that Ron could, seven years after his divorce, marry
me. He had described the searing pain of the divorce; the loss
of time with his children, then preadolescents; the destruc-
tion of his home, his vision for the future, his social circles.
I couldn't comprehend why God put these things in motion
so that I could finally have The One for whom I'd spent years

praying. Was finding each other across two thousand miles its own kind of miracle? How could all this loss be the answer to my supplication?

The answer, of course, is that God didn't pull a few strings, causing Ron's marriage to collapse so that we could fulfill destiny. Instead, God suffered alongside Ron and his first family, walking through the loss Ron felt and providing comfort with the help of his close friends. Together, God and Ron, with his children and his community, worked to redeem what was lost, and that redemption included meeting and marrying me. God wasn't trying to punish Ron or his first wife (or their kids), and God did not use the divorce to teach anyone a lesson. God didn't allow the divorce to happen so that God might be glorified. To believe that suggests we likewise believe that God favors those whose marriages are long-lasting, that God is discriminate in love, that God deems some folks more worthy of happiness, satisfaction, lack of discord. Given what the Bible shows us about the character of God, we must emphatically argue that any of the assumptions driving a blueprint theology are not true.

In some ways, the existence of my entire family has as its foundation one kind of loss or another: a divorce and remarriage, the loss of an intact family, the loss of birth cultures and birth families. All of us—my husband, my stepchildren, my two teenage sons—have tried to redeem some of that loss together, forging a new family that is unique, complicated, challenging, and beautiful. Despite the losses we have experienced, we are worthy of the love that God offers us and that we offer each other. This might feel a lot like a blessing to some people, but I can only say I am grateful.

Part III

WORTHY

9

THE CHURCH'S PROBLEM WITH THE BIG BUT

I still remember what the yellow school bus sounded like when it pulled up to our house in Illinois. How the green vinyl seats stuck to my legs in hot weather, and how the heater hummed beneath our feet in cold. For the first years of my education, I rode that bus across the town of Markham to attend the District Development Center, even though there was a public school closer to the parsonage where we lived. These were the early years of desegregation, and Markham was a mostly segregated town, a southern suburb of Chicago bisected by Kedzie Avenue. People who were black primarily lived on one side of Kedzie, and people who were white lived on the other.

At the time, I knew the general boundaries that Kedzie Avenue created, mostly because I was prohibited from crossing Kedzie, a busy thoroughfare, by myself to play with my best friend on the other side. I didn't know about desegregation or the Supreme Court ruling that had happened three years after my birth, establishing that busing could be legally used to desegregate schools. I didn't know why we took a bus to school, or that my parents—activists in the civil rights movement—had ensured our enrollment there. I didn't know about earlier court decisions that affirmed separate but equal was an unjust policy; or that most racially segregated institutions were definitely separate but *not* equal. I didn't know that some adults believed children who were white were considered more worthy of a good education than their peers who were black. All I knew was riding the bus to and from a school I loved, riding the bus especially into the long afternoons, because my brother and I were the last ones off.

More than forty years after school busing became one way to repudiate the divisiveness of "separate but equal," we continue to have a problem with that one word: *but*. It is so often used to establish division between those who are deemed worthy and those who are not. We make claims about people that are always accompanied by a "but": about the roles people play, about their bodies and minds, about God's love for them. We are surrounded by messages that tell us to accept and love ourselves . . . *but* to seek transformation, buy the next product, do the next self-help treatment, imbibe the next ideology to be truly accepted and loved. We have created institutions that perpetuate a sense of separate but definitely not equal, and our schools, government, entertainment industry, and churches are split along racial, gender, sexual, and socioeconomic lines. Those who have power often assert that this division, and the privilege it gives to some, is more about merit and hard work and biblical authority and God's goodness than it is, at times, about sheer dumb luck.

Creating a world where we can all find ourselves means challenging those with privilege who believe—in thought, language, and deed—that they are more worthy than others. It means challenging those messages that tell us we are not enough, just as we are. It means thinking about our big "but" problem and why we should say enough to the many expectations that tell us . . .

Love the sinner but hate the sin.

You are worthy just as you are, but you need to change.

You are fearfully, individually made, but you must conform to be accepted.

That one coordinating conjunction—*but*—manages to erase the value that exists in each statement's first clause. It's almost as if this is a zero-sum game, the initial phrase offering warm affirmation, and the second negating that affirmation completely. In the same way that "separate but equal" provided ample justification for some people to embrace segregation, the *but* in these phrases suggests validation while also condoning division. Ultimately, these statements are a way to keep distance from those who are judged to be living in sin and refusing to change and conform.

We need to attend to the church's big but problem.

Those who endorse such theology don't see it that way, of course. They believe the "but" is also important, even necessary, in conveying exactly what the Bible says. Biblical authority has become a way to sanctify the "but" that leads to separation. Consider these words from a prominent evangelical preacher, spoken on Easter Sunday in 1960: "All Orthodox, Bible-believing Christians agree on one thing; and that is, whatever the Bible says is so." The preacher admits that difference exists in how people interpret the Bible, and that this difference in interpretation is what causes "all the troubles we have today." If only people could see the Bible for its clearly stated truth in the Word of God, he says, all would be better. We have "ceased to believe in the authoritative Bible," and are beholden to darkness.[1]

In my adult life as a Christian, I've heard this claim on countless occasions. The Bible is treated as a transparent text that we only need read to understand. Those who disagree with an authority's interpretation are not Bible believers, are not aligned with the Truth, are not in God's will. People of faith who hope to condemn another group justify that group's exclusion by insisting that biblical authority demands exclusion. That the Bible itself champions separation. And that those who disagree about the Bible are obviously not seeing what is clearly written in Scripture.

But listen: On Easter Sunday in 1960, those words about the "authoritative Bible" and the need to do exactly what the Bible says? They were spoken by Bob Jones Sr., who was in the middle of a sermon about how the Bible demands racial segregation. According to Jones, the mixing of races in America upset an "established order," an order which held that blacks and whites were made—*in God's will*—to remain separated. In a carefully constructed argument, Jones affirmed that he had authority from the Bible, which endorses the "boundary of the nations," and that the mixing of races in America was Satan's work, carried out through the hands of communists and "religious liberals." Jones reminded his listeners that they needed to return to the Word, and that he understood the truth found in the Gospels in ways others could not.[2]

Jones's message is chilling because it preaches white supremacy couched as biblical truth. Racism is shot through this sermon preached on Easter morning, when Christians celebrate the power of light over darkness. It is also chilling because I hear echoes of the same language being used today by folks who believe with certainty that they know what the Bible teaches, and who suggest that the Bible teaches separating and excluding those deemed unworthy.

WHILE I WAS WRITING THIS BOOK, my church was dividing into two congregations. It had been splintering for years actually, falling apart despite the pastoral team's best efforts to hold the church and its people together. Behind-the-scenes alliances were formed, disparaging words were spoken, anger and judgment rained down on church leaders trying to keep the church from devolving into chaos. But the center could not hold. My church had countless meetings, listening sessions, prayer and discussion times to try to divine what its future should be and whether it should stay with a conference whose churches embrace a faith statement on human sexuality that condemns those who identify as LGBT. Our church had a few other options: to leave the conference and develop its own position on human sexuality, perhaps one that remained ambivalent about people who are LGBT, or to join a new conference, one that was welcoming and affirming. It was decided that those who disagree about human sexuality cannot remain in the same church. The congregation had decided this even though people in the church have disagreed for years about other important theological tenets, such as whether women can be in leadership or whether followers of Christ should believe in nonresistance. Human sexuality apparently trumped all. And now, after twenty years of attending a church where my children were dedicated, where they were raised from babies into teens, where we spent most every Sunday and every Christmas Eve worshiping with others: after all this, our church home doesn't exist anymore, even as the building still stands. The breakup has been even more painful for others, who were raised and married in the church, who mourned their parents' deaths in its pews, and who gave their lives and vocations to the church's ministry.

The story of my church is being replicated in congregations everywhere. People who have worshiped together for decades, raised kids together, and walked through dark places together have decided they can no longer tolerate difference. Or, really, one kind of difference, one based on the belief that some are worthy of inclusion and some are not. Others in my church would have framed this differently, of course: that our disagreement is about how we read Scripture, the ways we understand sin, how we see the role of grace and mercy, even the significance of science and whether people are born with sexual preference encoded or come by their sexuality through choice. All of this seems, to me, like noise keeping us from addressing the real issue. We believe some people deserve to be part of the church and some do not.

This current divisiveness is not new, a fact that Bob Jones Sr.'s 1960 Easter sermon makes stunningly clear. Those who have had power in the church have always drawn distinct lines between those who are worthy and those who are not. For several millennia, those in power decided that women were not worthy of God's vocational call to leadership, and that God preferred using men as God's envoys on earth. Not only preferred, but demanded it. The Bible, written by men in patriarchal societies and mostly interpreted by men, was seen to endorse the exclusion of women, deemed not worthy because of their presumably smaller brains, their simple minds, their genetic disposition that made them weaker, softer, docile. The white church similarly used its power to decide that people with white skin were more worthy than people of color; and that the Bible, written by powerful men in patriarchal societies, endorsed the exclusion and enslavement of others, deemed not worthy because of their presumably smaller brains, their simple minds, their genetic disposition that made them good workers but little else. The contemporary church has used its power to decide that people who are in relatively good mental health are more worthy than people with mental illness; and that the Bible, written by powerful men in patriarchal societies, endorses the exclusion of those deemed not worthy because of their presumed collusion with the devil or their seeming lack of moral fortitude.

I could go on. The church's history of exclusion is long.

But this history of exclusion—of finding some people unworthy—doesn't seem to match the vision offered us in the Gospels. There, Jesus sits alongside people who have been declared unworthy. Jesus regularly fellowshipped with women, who had little social standing in his time; he also communed with people who were beggars and tax collectors, prostitutes and blasphemers. The four Gospels narrate innumerable stories about Jesus' willingness to deconstruct the prominent hierarchy and then reconstruct another pattern of relating: one in which all are inherently worthy, in which all are welcomed at his table. Why we have refused to fully embrace this vision remains a mystery, unless we recognize that for too long, believing we are enough—truly enough— has meant also believing that others don't belong. It's an us-versus-them polarity that has devastated too many people for too long.

At some point, Christians really do need to say enough.

YES, BUT . . . people say, reminding us that divisions are often about the matter of sin, about who accepts grace and is redeemed and who continues to live "in sin." Back when I was attending a Christian college and lying about my own conversion story, I knew that those who received Jesus were expected to be unswayed by temptation, able to pass up donuts and beer, and inclined toward pure thought and speech. Those Big Jesus conversion stories also taught me that some sins mattered more than others, and that my peers had developed—thanks, I imagine, to their evangelical upbringings—a rubric for which sins were more deserving of God's grace. That rubric drove the testimonies they gave. Sexual sins were definitely at the top of this pecking order, although maybe they were not as dire as murder and other unsanctioned forms of violence. Substance abuse followed sex, which was followed by disobedience to authority, blatant unkindness toward family, and skipping church and youth group functions. No one would name this hierarchy, of course, but we all knew where we stood because of it: where we stood in our relationship to God, and in our relationship to others. The sins that tended to trip me up—gluttony, jealousy, and greed—held little purchase with the Christian crowds in which I ran, compelling me to dream up something bigger and more dastardly for my conversion story.

When we talk about inclusion in the church, too many people go directly to their rubrics, as if this assessment tool itself might decide who is worthy enough to be welcomed in the church and who is unworthy. Some will say that their rubrics are biblical, that they are founded on "what God wants," that the rubrics are objective and wise and loving. Writing teachers like me know that most rubrics are entirely subjective. What is considered unfathomable sin to some, is to others a simple expression of being who God created them to be. No matter. Exclusion using this unspoken rubric of sin is one more way those in power impose specific and rigid expectations on others, telling them exactly how they must act if they are to receive a passing grade and a ticket to the afterlife.

The damage, emotional and otherwise, wrought by those who apply the rubric of sin to others is clear. I think of teen mothers, learning that their sin of fornication makes them—and their offspring—unwelcome in their youth groups (which their baby daddies still attend). I think about women who are told that speaking in worship is sinful and wrong, learning that their voices do not matter. I think about people with mental illnesses who are told that their disordered brains are a manifestation of their sinfulness and their acquiescence to the devil, and are taught to feel shame for their cognitive differences and their "strange" behaviors. I think about transgender children, learning that their endeavors to live a gender different from the sex listed on their birth certificate are an aberration, that they are not worthy of accommodation. I think about gays and lesbians, their sexual identities so disgraceful that entire congregations (indeed, entire denominations) are willing to split rather than include them unconditionally.

Just about every semester, I abandon the rubrics I've used to assess students' essays, recognizing that everything I've thought about the old rubrics—about my assignments, the way I assess writing, the relative importance of writing elements—was all wrong, and that a new, better rubric is needed. I suggest we need to do the same for the rubrics by which we judge others, both the real and the imagined kinds, realizing that everything we've thought about expectations—about what we demand people act, think, and say—might in fact be wrong. This new rubric would have only one objective: ensuring that our expectation for others allows them to be exactly who God created them to be. Even when that be-ing makes them different from us. *Especially* when that be-ing makes them different from us.

Critics of this rubric might immediately resist, asserting that such an objective is too relative, that its standards lack biblical rigor, that there is no way to divine exactly what God wants for God's people. This is an interesting claim, given how much coin has been made by people declaring what God wants, then packaging it for our consumption. Sometimes the rhetoric of loving the sinner but hating the sin gets tossed around, an assertion that is far less loving when accompanied by the assertion that people need to change completely before they can be deemed worthy. When I think about the grand sweep of the Bible, its many contradicting narratives and the complexity of the text, I recognize that the Bible itself provides seemingly paradoxical messages about what God wants for God's people. But the overarching theme is one of love. It is the theme that ties together the Old and New Testaments, that grounded Jesus' ministry, that reflects the nature of God: this sense that God's love for us, and our love for each other, supersedes all, even our sense that a sinner needs to change to receive love, because God loves us no matter who we are. Unconditionally.

Of the many theories I learned about in graduate school, the one with the most staying power is that of "interpretive communities." Stanley Fish, a professor at Duke University, developed a reader-response theory of literature, one that asserts that we derive meaning from texts within specific cultural and social contexts and that our communities, also driven by cultural and social contexts, help shape the interpretation of a text—that is, the way a text is read and understood.

I've long believed that Fish's idea of interpretive communities illuminates the ways the Bible itself is understood, and that Scripture—like any other text—can only be interpreted through the lens of our cultural and social communities. This claim does not make the Bible or its truth relative and subjective. Instead, it helps us see the Bible as a rich, dynamic document, one that is open to interpretation and is shaped by a corporate understanding of its readers, instead of a top-down interpretation in which one person transmits the truths of a text to listeners. On occasions when I teach a literature course, I see the significant difference between these two approaches to texts. When classes are set up so that students need only know what *I* think about a text, they don't need to engage with the reading—or even read what I've assigned. If I can simply tell them what to believe, why should they work to figure it out? When classes are formed around interpretive communities, however, students are compelled to engage with a text, understand it more completely, and develop their own sense of its meaning, in concord with their peers.

Applied to the Bible, the idea of interpretive communities allows us to experience Scripture as a rich text that demands our attention and invites our interactions. And interpretive communities can give us this: even when different communities interpret the text differently, according to their social and cultural perspectives, we all share the belief that God is love, that the biblical narrative has as its overarching theme God's love for God's people. We can concur that in that nexus, where we all find agreement, we also find God's truth, even if different interpretive communities disagree about the particulars.

YES, BUT, some people will argue, what about the matter of sin? What are we to do about behaviors that separate us from God, that cause searing pain to others, that devastate people and communities? Given our fidelity to specific narratives that demand clear conversion moments, we may be inclined to decide that anyone who is mired in sin needs that Big Jesus Moment to be made pure and to sin no more. The piety of Christian culture seems to suggest as much, and our language and actions reveal that those who are deemed unredeemed are considered unworthy of inclusion.

In a letter addressing the division in the congregation of which I was a part for twenty years, pastor Gregg Koskela provides a compelling answer to the "Yes, but . . ." dilemma:

> The power of Christ's gospel is that "while we were still sinners, Christ died for us" (Romans 5:8). The power of the incarnation is that God took on frail, human, marginalized flesh, identified with us, embraced us in all our weakness, and redeemed us. The power of the cross is that once and for all, the sorrow and the sin and the scapegoating of all human experience was swallowed up by our suffering Savior. . . . Our salvation came because Jesus bore the wrath of the holiness purity system with his violent death. His death demonstrated that system's failure, by rejecting and crucifying God's Messiah.[3]

Koskela notes that the new world God creates is one of unity rather than separation. Jesus modeled this unity in his ministry on earth, showing that he came to abolish the systems that demanded exclusion. As Jesus' envoys here and now, we are to continue that work, challenging the narratives, the language, and the traditions that tell us some people are more worthy than others and that we need to keep ourselves separated from those who are different from us. We need to disrupt messages that tell us we must change if we want to avoid separation. We need to be ourselves—worthy—even when the world is demanding somebody else.

Back in 1973, when I stepped onto a school bus for the first time and crossed the asphalt barrier that was Kedzie Avenue, my parents were repudiating the message that some children were more worthy of an education than others. They were repudiating those who said biblical authority demanded that it was sinful to upset the established order, that races should not mix. Although my parents probably felt some trepidation in sending my brother and me across town, I imagine how much more fear parents on the other side of Kedzie must have felt when they put their babies on a bus. They knew their children were worthy of an education too, despite messages telling them that separate *but* equal was good enough and that God's established order meant their children needed to stay in "their place."

The Gospels remind us that Jesus' ministry upended any established order, any sense of who was worthy and who wasn't. Jesus asked followers to turn to the "least of these," because when we reach out to those who are considered unworthy, we are reaching out to Jesus. He demanded that we reject wealth and the accoutrements of power and taught that those who lack privilege will find God's favor. Jesus wanted us to overcome evil with good, to turn the other cheek when we are confronted with violence.

And yet Christians have added a big *but* to the central claims of Jesus' life on earth. Yes, but Jesus hated sin. Yes, but Jesus was living in a different place and time, and thus his judgments on wealth need to be understood within that context. Yes, but Jesus' death on the cross means that we also must reject those who reject his gift of salvation.

Imagine what might happen if we could demolish the *but* that separates people, creating a divide as seemingly impenetrable as Kedzie Avenue. Imagine what might happen if we would accept that Jesus' incarnation changed the sentence structure—and thus the power structure—of those messages telling us we need to change to be made worthy.

Imagine if we could simply say:

Love the sinner.

You are worthy just as you are.

You are fearfully, wonderfully made.

10

CHALLENGING MESSAGES AND CHANGING THE WORLD

In my last semester of college, my vocational aspirations to become a sports journalist were felled by a high school freshman wearing a blue leotard.

Becoming a well-known sports writer had not been a lifelong objective of mine. As a child, my career goals ranged from Olympic diver to seeing-eye-dog trainer to dairy farmer. One belly flop nixed my diving ambitions, and a Chihuahua named Bimbo with a particularly nasty case of mange disabused me of my dreams to work with animals. Finally, I landed on journalism as a worthy career, and as a senior at George Fox College in 1990, I had even found a real job, writing sports and feature stories for the local weekly.

My beat included high school wrestling, a big-time sport in our small-town world, where cutting weight still seems like a fun weekend activity for teen boys. At the 1990 Oregon state meet, I witnessed a ninety-five-pound freshman from Newberg lose a championship match to an older, slightly stronger rival. An athlete myself, I couldn't imagine the heady glory of placing second at the state level in one's freshman year. So when I cornered the young wrestler for an interview, I asked him how he felt about such a worthy accomplishment.

"How do you *think* I feel?" he said, looking up at my face and sneering. Then he shoved past me to gather his belongings and leave the arena.

My eyes welled with tears, and I hid behind my steno pad. An entitled ninety-five-pound freshman, wearing a blue leotard, had made me cry. The interview was over.

Turns out my journalism career was too.

As I made the hour-long drive back to Newberg, I realized that maybe I wasn't cut out for the journalist's life after all. I mean, if a kid could slay me with one comment, how would I ever be able to interview subjects when the stakes were much higher than a lightweight wrestling match? Mere months before graduation I was facing a career crisis. My panic was exacerbated because I also hadn't landed a fiancé, the presumed goal of every Christian college senior. No career, no spouse, no idea what was happening next: I sobbed all the way home from Portland, my cheap Chevy Sprint reminding me that I was also graduating dirt poor.

Several weeks later I was crying again, this time in my academic advisor's office. Ed had been one of my favorite professors, a charismatic hippy with long hair and an earring, both anomalies for professors at my evangelical Christian college—his appearance as dissonant as the metallic-blue 1970 Pinto station wagon Ed drove to work each day. Ed made standing on desks popular long before Robin Williams did so in *Dead Poets Society*, and his teaching toolbox included throwing erasers at students, reading subversive poetry, and inspiring nascent writers by publicly ridiculing their appalling use of religious clichés.

In the weeks after deciding I couldn't be a journalist, I'd concluded I wanted to be an English professor just like Ed. I knew nothing about the deplorable job market for humanities educators or the extra schooling I'd need to earn a PhD. So I'd gone to consult with Ed, letting him know about my new vocational goal. Even though I wanted to be a teacher, I told him, I worried that my early struggles as a student and my shyness would make the job nearly impossible. I had discovered success in academics rather late in my young life, and I was wholly unlike other English majors, who seemed born knowing how to read. Besides, I told Ed, I couldn't fathom having to stand in front of crowds, or doing the classroom theatrics Ed seemed to enjoy. How would I ever be successful, given that I could never quote endless lines of my favorite childhood poems or come up with teaching strategies anything like those of my very flamboyant, extroverted professor?

"No!" Ed howled, pointing his finger straight at my face. "If you are going to be a professor, you will need to be you. Not me. Not some other professor. You will have to be who you are."

Twenty-some years into a very happy teaching career, I am grateful for that skinny wrestler in a blue leotard, and for my hippy professor, and for finding my place vocationally. I cannot imagine doing anything else—including writing newspaper stories about the still-successful Newberg wrestling program. There were plenty of other rabbit trails on my way to becoming a professor, because I couldn't really believe that God wanted me to teach. I tried my hand at doing urban relief work with the elderly, serving as an aide at a school for students with mental illnesses, and planting flowers on a landscaping crew in the oppressive midwestern heat. I kept coming back to what I felt was my calling to become a college professor, remembering Ed's exhortation that I needed to be who *I* was, not what I believed everyone else expected a good professor to be. Somewhere along the way, I earned a doctorate in English, found a spouse, and brought home my first puppy, a black lab named Flannery who was unlike Bimbo in every way possible.

Of course, some days I still wonder if I'm living up to expectations people have about college professors. I don't cherish the life of the mind like many of my colleagues do, and I still worry that my learning deficits as a child are glaringly obvious to my peers and to my students. Most nights I still prefer watching television to reading academic essays, and sometimes my inability to spell simple words and my lack of knowledge about grammar rules is a crying shame. Twenty years into my teaching career, though, I know that being an English professor is what I'm called to do, even if I still don't dance on desktops or throw erasers at students. I'm being the professor I know God created me to be.

I imagine Ed didn't intend to change the world when I came to his office that rainy winter afternoon in 1990. Knowing Ed as I do, it's easy to think he was slightly annoyed by my knock on his office door, and that he was distracted by a million other things waiting for him at his hobby farm outside town: the llamas he needed to feed, the goats he needed to milk, the dinner in need of cooking. Putting all his pressing chores aside, Ed gave me thirty minutes of his time and attention, challenging my deepest-held convictions about my vocation and about his. And because of that one conversation, my life direction was completely changed.

By challenging the messages I'd heard, Ed changed my world.

Not every encounter we have will be so life-shattering, and not every student who visited Ed's office (or, these days, mine) will have a mind-blowing epiphany. But the possibility exists that each time we interact with others, we have an amazing opportunity to acknowledge that we are all fearfully, wonderfully made; and we have the chance to call forth that which makes us each an image-bearer of God. We really do have a chance to change the world, one interaction at a time.

SOMETIMES, our interactions will be not around vocation or calling, but around a text that is fundamental to our faith. Changing the world we live in and finding ourselves worthy might mean acknowledging that the Bible—and, really, the name of God—is used to dehumanize others, to deny them basic human rights, to put people in their place by implying that they are not worthy of God's love, God's grace, God's mercy.

I once got in a heated argument with a college roommate about the authority of the Bible. Or rather, the authority of *my* Bible, which she'd been monitoring for weeks and weeks, noticing that it hadn't been opened or moved, evidence that I didn't take the Bible seriously, and that thus my theology was suspect. The discussion grew out of a disagreement about the Iran-Contra hearings (which sounds far more cerebral than it actually was) and my insistence that Jesus abhorred war and called us all to be pacifists. I was really getting my Mennonite on, echoing the ideology I'd learned as a child about Jesus' Sermon on the Mount and the case for nonresistance found in the Gospels, when my roommate chastised me for not reading my Bible enough to have any authority about its contents. She'd been watching.

Although I was annoyed that she would keep track of my Bible (and actually, still am . . .), my own behavior mimicked that of far too many Christians, then and now, who rely on the authority of the Bible and the assurance of what it says without truly engaging with the text. Our Bibles grow dusty and unopened even as we proclaim the significance of the text in guiding our every decision. The general biblical illiteracy of many Western Christians is one marker of how little we actually know the Bible's contents. According to some surveys, many Christians cannot even name more than five commandments, let alone know why the story of Tamar is such a chilling one. Instead, too many of us proclaim with certainty that the Bible affirms a specific, well-defined worldview; one prominent Christian publication even called its journalism "biblical objectivity" because it is so certain the Bible is transparent and objective about all things.[1]

The very idea of biblical objectivity seems problematic to me. I imagine that if the Bible were more transparent, there wouldn't be so many Christian denominations that have split over and over again about what the Bible *really* says and how we are to interpret biblical authority in the first place. And often the Bible is used as a kind of trump card, plunked into a debate as if we are to accept, without question, the biblical premise being offered. You know, "The Bible says it, I believe it, that settles it"—even when the "it" isn't clearly defined. Read most any comments section of a religious publication and you will see this game played out, with "According to the Bible . . ." being served in generous helpings, as if a person's interpretation solves a complicated, nuanced argument once and for all.

What would happen, though, if we made space for each other to question what the Bible really says, to challenge suppositions about the Bible, to think about the biblical narratives we've been told (some of us since childhood) and wonder about how we might understand those narratives differently? To do so might help us see that presumed "biblical" expectations are not so biblical after all. To do so might help us feel free to become the unique people God has created us to be.

Kendra Weddle Irons, a professor of religion at Texas Wesleyan University, has helped countless students (and me, her coauthor for *If Eve Only Knew*) reimagine and understand the Bible in new ways. She feels called to erase presuppositions and expectations about what it means to be a "biblical woman," providing space for many to approach Scripture in a holistic way that is refreshing and life-giving. In her classes and seminars, Irons often challenges others to listen closely to biblical stories by asking them to imagine what the stories' characters were thinking and feeling at the time, and she provides cultural and historical contexts to help with this imagining. The story about Jesus' healing of a bleeding woman is one such example.

Normally, teachings about this story focus on Jesus and the healing, but Irons wants readers to wonder what the experience must have been like for the woman, ostracized because of her illness and bleeding in a culture where she would have been considered unclean. If this story was intended to be about only the healing, Irons says, it would end after the woman is made well. But the story continues: Jesus wants to know who touched his garment, and seeks the woman out in the crowd. According to purity laws of the time, Jesus has now also become unclean. In recognizing the woman, he also acknowledges his uncleanliness; in doing so, he challenges conventional thinking about purity, the unjust treatment of the bleeding woman, and the oppression she experienced because she was a woman, was poor, was ill. As Irons and I write in *If Eve Only Knew*, "rather than succumbing to the injustice created by well-intentioned laws, Jesus modeled compassion for those most negatively affected by religious stipulations. . . . By bringing their exchange into public view, Jesus showed people are more important than systems, that compassion rather than judgment was the appropriate response to those marginalized by society."[2]

In pushing against predominant interpretations of this story, Irons helps readers see a different dynamic in Jesus' ministry, one intent on removing unjust barriers in his culture—in this case, the restrictive purity laws—that limited people, often in dramatic ways.

Changing the world means being willing to challenge expectations established with the phrase "the Bible says," as if the Bible is absolutely clear on most matters. As Irons does with her students, interrogating the Bible means seeing its stories from multiple perspectives and asking how those different viewpoints might alter and deepen our understanding of Scripture. It also means looking to the life of Jesus as a model for how we treat others, rather than using scriptural sound bites to justify behavior. Writing for *Sojourners* magazine, Stephen Mattson critiques those who would "exploit scripture in the name of Jesus" by using the Bible to justify behavior that seems contradictory to the life and ministry of Jesus. Given our current cultural climate, Mattson says, Christians "commit all sorts of theological gymnastics to rationalize doing just the opposite" of what Jesus said about loving neighbors and praying for those who are meek, or poor, or downtrodden. Instead, they "propagat[e] doctrinal arguments that successfully pretend to be Christ-like while in reality circumventing Jesus almost entirely."[3] We may, for example, be told that the Bible demands that men have authority over women and that women should not be permitted to lead, and we may be told these precepts are "biblical." But the life of Christ sets up a different model for women as well as different expectations for how women are to be treated in the public and private sphere. It is Jesus himself who makes us free from "biblical" expectations.

I recently read a blog post by a student who identifies as LGBT and who wrote about the painful experience of having been scorned by Christians. Someone commented on the post that the writer needed to "follow the way of scripture, rather than the way of the world." The false dichotomy suggests there is only one way to read Scripture, and that those who disagree with that reading are only capitulating to "the world" and its values. I want to say to the student who shared her deepest pain—and to the anonymous commenter who used the Bible as a scolding mechanism—that the way of Scripture is not a clearly demarcated path, and that it is our job to forge a road forward together. We need to ask hard questions about the Gospels. To interrogate the ofttimes puzzling nature of Jesus' ministry. To acknowledge that Jesus stood with the marginalized, not those in power. To recognize that the Bible's grand narrative tells us we are all worthy of God's love and grace.

RIGHT NOW, it feels as though—in North America at least—
we live in a world beset by incivility and division. Everyone is
divided along all kinds of fault lines. In the journalism classes
I teach, we talk regularly about how the media feeds our division, as most of us choose to be informed by those outlets that
only confirm, rather than challenge, our biases. These days we
live in echo chambers, letting us believe exactly what we want
to believe: that those who live on the other side of the divide
are less human, less worthy, than we are. We can't even log on
to social media without feeling the full effect of this division.

The church has not been immune to this divisiveness.
Except, in churches, these arguments take on a different hue,
and although they are often no more civil than other discussions, they often devolve into disagreements about how we read
Scripture, and also *what* we read in Scripture. To call a fellow
Christian out for not "following biblical authority" becomes
in its own way a biting invective used uncivilly to silence those
with whom we disagree.

To suggest that we need to argue *more* might, at first blush,
seem like adding fuel to an already flaming heap of angry Facebook rants, online screeds, church schisms. But there are times
when we are called to argue more, to challenge the narratives,
the language, the family and church traditions, and the cultural
messages that tell us conformity is preferred to individuality.
When we are consistently bombarded with messages about our
unworthiness, having the energy to respond is difficult, but it is
also essential if we are to form communities where we are, all
of us, accepted just as we are.

In the Gospels, Jesus challenges his followers again and
again to give up all they have to follow him. Jesus tells a rich
man that to be perfect, he must sell his possessions, give that

income to the poor, and then follow him (Matthew 19:21). We are told that we must renounce our families—even hate our mothers and fathers—if we want to become a disciple of Jesus (Luke 14:26). When Jesus meets Simon Peter, James, and John, he tells them to drop everything if they wish to become fishers of humanity, and they do (Luke 5). These stories are unsettling, because they suggest an unalloyed release of everything we hold dear if we wish to be true followers of Jesus.

That release needs to include the tight grasp we have on those things that have made us comfortable: the ways we've looked at and understood the world; the ways we've traditionally understood Scripture; and thus the ways we've continually divided ourselves between those who are worthy and those who are not. This notion is particularly unsettling, because it seems that we are faced with one more expectation: to sacrifice everything we've known and owned to follow Jesus. My first compulsion is to hold on to these things just a little tighter, to ask Jesus whether he really means that we sacrifice *all*. But I know the answer, and I know I have also failed to give up all I've learned and believed for the sake of serving and loving Jesus.

Changing the world sometimes takes sacrifice, a willingness to argue against our most comfortable assumptions, including those labeled "biblical." And while social media posts give us a ready platform to argue our views and challenge others' belief systems, it seems that Jesus is asking us for much more. We might need to log off Facebook and step into the real world, especially if we want equity to reign on earth as in heaven.

When I think of world-changers, I think of the makers of justice in my own life, those who have argued against expectations, often at significant cost.

I think of my friend Kendra Weddle Irons, arguing that we need a different lens through which to understand the Bible, one that asks us to see Scripture as a dynamic text God uses to speak to us about love, not as a list of prohibitions or a user's manual for the good life. Kendra's willingness to interrogate the Bible has not always been comfortable or easy, especially in the early years of her career. Arguing for a different view of the Bible put her vocation at risk: university administrators were leery of giving tenure to a teacher whose views would be especially challenging to evangelical undergraduates. She persisted, though, and many young people in her classes heard for the first time that God wanted women to also use their gifts of speaking, preaching, leading. Kendra challenged messages, and changed the world.

And I think of my friend Leslie, who risks relationships with others when she advocates for person-first language. I've seen her call out people who unthinkingly drop the R-word, telling them directly that such descriptors for others are unaccept-able, always. In our local school district, Leslie has worked tirelessly for the rights of students with disabilities, showing school administrators how inequities in resources convey to some families that their children are less worthy than others. Leslie continues to challenge messages about what it means to live with disabilities, and is changing the world.

I think of Shaylene, a Muslim American woman active in Portland's interfaith community who forges relationships with Christians and Jews because she knows that doing so is one way to heal religious divides in her community. Last year, Shaylene enrolled in a community police officer program, aware that Muslims in North America are often stereotyped; she wanted to ensure that police in her community had a connection to the Muslims they served. Although some in her mosque might resist her efforts, Shaylene is challenging messages about religious minorities in Oregon, and is changing the world.

I'm reminded of countless others who are doing the same: My brother-in-law, who quit a lucrative corporate job to work for the Peanut Butter Project, which focuses on providing nutrition in several West African countries, letting children there know they are worthy of life and health. Marg, a talented musician and Web designer, who is creating bridges between LGBT folks and Christians despite a lifetime of being rejected by Christians, often in painful ways. Jennifer, who has moved several times in the last few years but finds avenues to support the undocumented immigrants in each community she joins. And countless former students who, in ways big and small, are putting aside their own agendas and finding courage to argue that those without voices deserve to be heard.

They are taking seriously the call to relinquish what they hold dear for the sake of others. They are challenging those messages that say some are worthy and others are not. They are changing the world.

AT THE UNIVERSITY WHERE I TEACH, having a diverse student population has been a priority as well as a challenge for the administration. Although the situation is improving and George Fox University now has a student body that is marginally diverse in its racial makeup, there are classes in which I see only two or three people of color in a sea of white faces. Some students have shared with me what it's like to be a racial minority at my institution—for example, what it feels like to be pressed to speak on behalf of an entire racial or ethnic group in classes or to have professors ask directly, "Has this been your experience, as a person of color?"

I know how inappropriate such questions can be, because I know a bit about what it means to be that person, carrying the weight of an entire people group on her back. I've been the token tenured woman on committees, supposedly representing all women faculty, or the token woman on a speaker's dais, showing that an institution accepts women in leadership. Yet I also know that my privilege means I have a luxury not afforded my students who are minorities because of their socioeconomic, racial, gender, religious, or sexual identities. That is, despite the evangelical culture where I work, I have the luxury to share my life experiences with very little risk of censure (or worse). For many of my students, this is not the case, and there can be a significant cost to pushing back against expectations that demand they act, think, or be someone different from what and who they are.

While I want to rush headlong into confrontations on behalf of those who are powerless, I need to recognize that changing the world sometimes means being quiet so that others can speak. In a lot of ways, being quiet is something I'm good at; as an introvert, it's easy for me to fade into the background of any social situation, allowing other people to talk and fill up the space I've vacated. Often, though, I'm not good at being silent, especially when an argument erupts on social media and I feel righteous outrage, wanting to defend a person whose point of view is underrepresented or marginalized. And when I believe my views are under attack, it's easy for me to summon the courage to speak up rather than listen, although sometimes—if I'm honest—this courage emerges out of my desire to defend myself from accusations of white privilege.

"I'm not that way at all!" I feel inclined to protest whenever someone posts on Facebook or a student suggests that white privilege has blinded me and others to systemic racism. How can I be racist, I might plead, especially because I have two sons who are people of color?

Stop. That question, rattling through my head, always stops me, perhaps because I've seen it used in one form or another to justify racism ("I have black friends, so how can I be a racist?"); to justify sexism ("I love my wife and daughters and treat them well, so how can I be sexist?"); to justify discrimination against those who are LGBT ("My colleague is gay, and we get along great! How can I be a bigot?"). When we are inclined to justify our exclusion of others in this way, the best thing we can do—the most freeing act we can make—is to stop, be quiet, and hear the stories of others. Challenging messages and changing the world might, at times, require that we resist defending our points of privilege and simply listen to what others might be telling us about their experiences, about the expectations they face. By being silent, by actively listening to others' stories, we are affirming that their stories—indeed, their *lives*—truly matter, and that they are worthy by virtue of their human experience, nothing more or less.

Once we check our privilege and truly listen to the stories of another, we can act together to change the world we inhabit, following the lead of those who know best what a community needs and how we can help. Those who have been marginalized should not have to do this world-changing work themselves, and it is up to those who live with privilege to work alongside those on the margins, creating together a place where equity reigns. People should not have to seek justice for their communities on their own. But they should also have space and a platform to tell their own stories.

Even though she is writing from a different cultural perspective and specifically about LGBT people, Roxane Gay, in *Bad Feminist*, addresses this notion by saying, "Despite our complex cultural climate and what needs to be done for the greater good, it is still an unreasonable burden that someone who is marginalized must bear an extra set of responsibilities." It is unfair, Gay writes, for us to expect well-known people who identify as LGBT to "forge inroads" on behalf of everyone else who also identifies as such, doing the work of justice "to change the world, to carry the burdens we are unwilling to shoulder, to take the stands we are unwilling to make."[4] When I read this, I think about the times I haven't acted alongside people who are marginalized because their battles are not my own. I think about my students who are religious, racial, or sexual minorities, and upon whom we tend to foist the expectation to take a stand on their own for their rights, or to explain to everyone else what it feels like to be them. I think of friends who have children with disabilities and who must fight alone against the expectations, systemic and otherwise, that say those with disabilities are not worthy of full inclusion. I think of all the ways my own silence can be complicity, a barrier to which I unintentionally contribute, keeping people who are marginalized from being who God created them to be—or conversely, the ways that my rush to speak has silenced others, not giving them space to tell their own stories about expectation and unworthiness.

Challenging expectations that have limited my potential has been difficult enough; challenging those that limit others can feel too overwhelming a task. How do I push back against all those expectations, when they emerge from everywhere, so much a part of our culture that it seems as though we live and breathe messages telling us we are not worthy? What should my response to widespread injustice be, especially given my own privilege? Do I speak, or do I stay silent?

To what does God call me?

Bad Feminist provides some answers to these questions. Gay writes that we need to acknowledge our privilege, even when it seems as though we have no privilege. And we need to use our privilege, if only in small ways, to help make inroads toward justice, taking up some of the burden others have carried on their own for too long. For Gay, this might mean voting for politicians who will work for justice, and protesting those who do not. This might mean calling out language and narratives that limit others from reaching their potential. This might mean challenging popular culture that serves to demean women; Gay mentions withholding support from rappers like Tyler the Creator, whose music includes the lyrics "rape a pregnant [pejorative for a woman] and tell my friends I had a threesome," among other misogynist allusions. These acts might not seem like much, but, Gay writes, "there are injustices great and small, and even if we can only fight the small ones, at least we are fighting."[5]

For Christians, justice work must also mean challenging folks who assert, without evidence, that their ideologies are "biblical" or that their actions are part of "God's will." Such phrases are so facilely uttered in our churches and Christian institutions that we rarely take time to ask whether something *really is* biblical and whether some event that seems deeply tragic and horrible can *really* be God's will. Several years ago, during prayer at a church meeting, a man offered praise to

Syria's president Bashar al-Assad because he was, the man said, doing God's will—this despite Assad's notorious record of human rights abuses and the slaughter of his own people. I was appalled, but I didn't have the courage to challenge the man, even as I wondered how the death of so many innocents in Syria might have been God's will. Anointing events as "God's will" has become a normal part of political conversation, a rhetorical move that serves to silence those who disagree. How can we argue with the Bible, or with something that's been established as God's doing?

Justice work begins here: with the simple act of challenging the messages we receive about what it means to be fully human. And then deconstructing those messages that demand we change our essential selves if we want to be considered worthy. And then affirming, for ourselves and for each other, that we are fearfully, wonderfully, uniquely made. And, further, if I want to change the world to a place where all are deemed worthy, I will need to know when I should use my voice to ask questions and to argue, and when I should stay silent, creating space for someone else to use her voice. Changing the world requires that we ask the fundamental question: As someone who follows Jesus, to what work does God call me?

This is something with which we all must wrestle.

11

REDEEMING A NOT-SO-SWEET SIXTEENTH

My friends threw a sweet sixteen birthday party for me in 2014. I was forty-six years old.

Like most teen birthday parties, we celebrated with pizza, candy, and soda pop, plus a few adult beverages my friends snuck in. We played loud music from the '80s. Someone laminated a poster of my teen heartthrob (Alan Alda—don't ask) and we played a rowdy game that required a blindfold, lipstick, and kissing practice on Alan Alda's foxy face. I received gifts of *Teen Beat* magazine, nail polish, a diary, cola-flavored Lip Smackers. My friends made a cake, lit sixteen candles, sang "Happy Birthday." When these lovely women, my people, sang, I began to cry. And then laughed at my tears. And then cried some more.

On that warm late-summer night, my friends managed to redeem a horrible experience I had when I actually did turn sixteen—an experience that left me feeling, for about thirty years, that I was not worthy of people's time, attention, or love. Back in 1984, on the date of my first sixteenth birthday party, no one showed up. Not one person. I had waited on our porch for friends to arrive at seven o'clock, but then the calls started coming in, people sending their regrets. Others never bothered to call at all. Finally, at seven forty-five, when it was clear no one was coming, I pulled the candles from the cake, helped my mom put away the party supplies, and tried not to feel completely devastated, even though I was.

A sixteenth birthday party isn't a huge deal, not in the scheme of things. But for me, the magnitude of that rejection, coupled with other slights big and small, has lingered for decades. So when a few friends offered to throw me a sixteen (plus thirty) party, I hesitated. Could I risk the potential of having my heart broken again? What if no one showed up, again? Why would anyone want to celebrate me, anyway? All the messages about myself I'd internalized over the years—that I was unlovable, uninteresting, unworthy—were distilled into this one defining moment thirty years ago.

That moment was redeemed, thirty years later, when a bunch of people decided that despite their own plans—their jobs, their families, their busy lives—I was important enough to celebrate.

I always thought I was alone in my sixteenth birthday embarrassment, that everyone else I knew probably had raucous sweet sixteenths with massive groups of rowdy teenagers partying late into the night, à la '80s-era John Hughes movies and MTV. But when a friend wrote a blog post about my forty-sixth birthday party, a number of comments suggested that I was not alone after all. That, in fact, many people carry the weight of disappointment and rejection, sometimes because no one showed up for a party, a baby shower, a wedding reception, or—even more devastatingly—when no one showed up, period, to support someone who was floundering.

The truth is, most of us walk through life burdened by our sense that we are not worthy, and that something essential needs to change about ourselves before we will be loved and accepted. Many of us are devastated by life events that remind us of our unworthiness, a devastation compounded by messages from our families, our churches, our culture that tell us that we are not enough. I imagine many us are like my sixteen-year-old self, sitting on the front porch, waiting for folks to arrive. When no one comes, we believe—for hours, days, thirty years, forever—that the space we occupy in the world doesn't matter so much after all.

So this is what a community can do for you: it can remind you that you are loved. It can deconstruct those many messages saying that you must change to be acceptable, and then can reconstruct another narrative, one that acknowledges you as a unique, beautiful, wonderful image-bearer of God. It can celebrate you with cake and punch and (if needed) a poster-sized picture of Alan Alda. A good community can let you know that your presence matters in the world, to the people around you, to God.

A community lets you know you are worthy, just as you are.

For too many people, this kind of affirmation seems to come too late. Funerals and memorial services sometimes seem to be the only times where people are truly feted, their goodness lauded for a gathered crowd. This is a literal and figurative crying shame, and I wish everyone who felt themselves unworthy might experience what I did at my sweet sixteen party, when my perfect community of less-than-perfect people told me I was loved.

FINDING SUCH A SUPPORTIVE COMMUNITY can be exceedingly difficult, something I encountered for long stretches of my life, including my years in graduate school, when I was far away from home, had a small, dumpy apartment to myself, and studied an unconscionable amount every day. Because I knew during that time that my state of loneliness was temporary—I would graduate someday, after all—my first decade as a mother actually seemed even more isolating. During those early years of motherhood, I lived a long loneliness as a working mom at an evangelical college in a small, predominantly conservative town. Many of the mothers I knew stayed at home to care for their children, had playdates together during the day, and gathered for coffee when their kids were old enough for preschool. Even though the church I attended had a women's Bible study, this was always scheduled at ten in the morning on Thursdays, when most working moms like me could not attend.

So I felt alienated from mothers in the community, and I also didn't really fit in at my institution, where—at least when my kids were young—only a handful of other mothers, scattered across campus, also worked in a full-time capacity. Many of my male colleagues could gather together for lunch in the cafeteria, fostering friendships over sandwiches and salads, while I ate lunch hunched at my desk, working. There were only so many hours in a day when I could be at work, undistracted by children. Calculating that a leisurely lunch with friends would cost me twenty bucks in childcare plus the cost of a meal, I often chose to grade essays in my office. I also chose loneliness, not only for me but also for my kids, who didn't have the play-dates other kids were privy to.

I know that other people have felt this aching aloneness, this sense that everyone else is having a raucous party with rich, abiding friendships, this fear of missing out on all that is right and good and beautiful about relationships. (There is even an acronym for this kind of fear-of-missing-out loneli-ness: FOMO.) I know that circumstances and life choices can isolate people, making them feel unworthy of good friendship, of the close, loving community that everyone deserves. I know how the lack of community can make people believe they are unlovable, and I even know how our cultures can exacerbate the sense that there is something wrong with a person who doesn't have a good support system. The church has done an especially good job of ensuring that those who don't fit into its "biblically" labeled boxes remain alone on the outside rather than drawn in and supported. Popular culture feeds us a con-sistent stream of images, telling us that connected people are more beautiful, more acceptable, more lovable than the rest of us, so much so that I've sometimes stopped watching tele-vision or looking at my Facebook account for long stretches because doing so makes me feel lonely all over again. So many happy people doing life in vivid, amazing ways while I sit on my futon, eating a sleeve of Oreos alone.

When I say that I have known intense loneliness, I really mean this. And then that loneliness was redeemed by women scattered across the country, members of a group called Chris-tian Feminism Today who encouraged me to be who God created me to be by simply being myself. Because my church was just one more space where I felt unworthy, the people in this organization became church for me, my time with them sacred and holy in ways my experiences in church never had been. Members of Christian Feminism Today, an ecumenical group of about 150 women and men dedicated to following Jesus, gather for a long weekend every other year to fellowship, learn from each other, and promote the cause of gender equity. The first time I attended this gathering, in 2012, I met women who from that point forward served as activist mothers for me, igniting my own passion for Jesus and my sense that the Bible calls us to justice. Many of the women had been feminists for forty or fifty years, part of the second wave of activism that had opened doors for my generational sisters and for me. Many had experienced discrimination firsthand in the church and in their families and could not fully stanch the deep wounds caused by cultural misogyny.

Over the course of one weekend with these new friends, I had found my people. They got me. They encouraged me to keep writing and teaching, reminding me that being a wife and mother were not the only roles God had given me and that I should not apologize for my decision to work outside the home. I listened to their stories and found strength in their strength, their willingness to persist despite hearing that women couldn't be leaders in the church, that women's voices were insignificant. The conference sessions repudiated this, celebrating the sacred beauty found in every woman, a recognition of our likeness to Mary, who participated in the incarnation. I cried my way through the final worship service. The liturgy's inclusive language welcomed me, and the communion tied me to women who were still strangers but sisters and mothers too. I had never experienced anything like this, and was reborn.

Because Christian Feminism Today is a nationwide organization and we only meet biannually, I don't see these people often. But I know they are there, offering unalloyed support via an email group where people request prayers, discuss the current cultural climate, and cheer on those who are excelling in their careers and celebrating life milestones like the birth of a grandchild or a marriage. When we talk about welcoming and inclusive church groups, I think first of these people from an array of religious traditions deciding that they will welcome all, including gays and lesbians who have been cast out of other churches and families. The Christian Feminism Today group emphatically models God's grace without judgment, and I'm grateful that they have become my people, because through them my life has been transformed.

Part of this transformation has included having the courage to find other communities closer to home. Feeling the love and support of my feminist friends, I was emboldened to find similar groups in my geographical area, and was more ready to lean into communities and friendships that had seemed too risky a few short years before. The book group that had at one time stoked my mothering guilt became a safe place for me to admit it, not because the people in the group had changed—for the most part, the group comprised the same women—but because my perspective had shifted. By rejecting those messages telling me exactly who Christian mothers should be, I could more clearly see the grace, rather than judgment, that these book club women offered me. In my vocation, I started to challenge my sense that I wasn't academic enough or smart enough or authoritative enough to relate to my colleagues. And once I dismissed messages about my embodied self that were not only culturally constructed but also patently false, I joined a gym, a serendipitous decision that has given me close friends, people who truly encourage me, in body and mind.

This is what powerful communities can do. By allowing people to be exactly who they are, powerful communities can also transform people, making them stronger and more whole than before. It's a beautiful paradox: we are changed when we are given permission to be the same. We become more of who God created us to be by accepting that God created us to be who we are, as we are.

Any group that works toward justice will have a similar message, and will work hard to ensure that people can be transformed by freeing them to be exactly who they are. Those working on behalf of people who identify as LGBT, of people who have disabilities, of people who experience socioeconomic injustice, of people who are oppressed and suppressed because they don't fit our societal perceptions of "normal": those doing justice for these people groups are affirming that people are inherently worthy, despite their differences. Given this fundamental belief, it becomes easy—necessary even—to go about challenging the images, the language, the narratives, the mythologies that demand that all differences be blunted away to the point that everyone looks, talks, thinks, acts the same way.

Sheryl Sandberg and Adam Grant, in their 2017 book, *Option B*, describe the power of rewriting narratives that limit people, suggesting that pushing back against predominant stories can help build resilience and community where it is needed most. They write, "Narratives might sound 'light'—how important can a story be?—but they are how we explain our past and set expectations for our future. . . . Shared stories are often created by rewriting old narratives and countering unfair stereotypes."[1] Sandberg believed so strongly in the importance of story as a way to build community that she built Lean In Circles (a concept based on her 2013 book, *Lean In*), where women create communities as a means of sharing their stories, countering injustice, and empowering each other. After just a few years, over thirty thousand circles exist in 150 countries, giving women collective strength by reminding them they are inherently worthy.[2]

Real justice work acknowledges this worthiness, then goes about destroying barriers that keep people from being who God created them to be. This may seem a simplistic distillation, but think about any justice movement in recent history and you will see this dynamic unwind—and always within the context of community. Those fighting for gender justice needed to first claim that women were fully human, that they were image-bearers of the divine, and that they deserved equal rights in every aspect of their lives. Once that truth was proclaimed, those working in concord needed to knock down the many barriers that have stood in the way of women's progress toward full inclusion, including laws that unfairly limit women; institutionalized misogyny that means a woman has to work significantly more for the same pay and career advancement; and theologies that demand women must stay silent, submissive, and cloistered at home. My Christian feminist people have been doing this work for several decades. Yet women continue to hear messages telling them they are not worthy, and there are still barriers keeping women from feeling fully accepted, in the church and elsewhere.

So there is still work to be done. And there are still people who need a community to show up, telling them they are loved.

Doing this is difficult, especially when we've found and want to hold tight to our own, when our community is a comfortable place to be who we were meant to be. I'm not sure God has called us to be comfortable, though. The writer Ana Marie Cox suggests that comfort is the province of the privileged, and that only those with privilege—however it is manifested—have the freedom to absolve themselves of uncomfortable situations and conversations.[3] This includes the discomfort that can come from reaching out to those who are marginalized, initiating conversation, inviting others to the center of our communities, and asking them to stay.

WHEN I WAS A CHILD, my parents modeled this for me every holiday by welcoming to our home those who didn't have another place to be. Sometimes, the collection of folks at our holiday table made dinner exceptionally uncomfortable, and I sometimes seethed with resentment because my parents had ruined my dinner by inviting in strangers who rambled in conversation, ate too loudly, or made puzzling declarations. I couldn't wait until the meal was over and my siblings and I could disappear to a bedroom to watch TV and laugh at the weird people still sitting at our dining room table.

I wish I could tell my teenage self to be far more loving, more grace-filled, for the decisions my parents had made. At that age and lacking a fully developed frontal lobe, I couldn't make the connection between the isolation our guests likely felt and the loneliness I experienced often during high school, including when an entire friend group rejected me on my birthday. I also couldn't see the love my parents were extending by providing community for those who had been told, throughout their lives and for many reasons, that they were not worthy of acceptance. Holiday meals would have been easier and more comfortable for my parents, too, if we hadn't hosted so many others. But my parents modeled the hard work of being uncomfortable for the sake of those who needed to belong.

When we can embrace the Bible's promise that we are fearfully, wonderfully, individually made, we can begin to convey that assurance to others as well, creating the kind of community that lets others know they are inherently worthy of inclusion, no matter who they are. Jesus' life and ministry reminds us that we are called to reach out to those who are waiting on their front steps, certain they are not worthy of a sixteenth birthday celebration. Perhaps I resonate with the parable of the great banquet in Luke 14 because of my own party experience. In the parable, a man creates an elegant banquet for his friends, but when everything is ready, no one can come, citing personal and professional obligations that make them too busy to attend. So the man tells his servants to go into the city and invite to the table those who are poor, or have disabilities, or are otherwise marginalized. "For I tell you," the man says, "none of those who were invited will taste my dinner" (Luke 14:24). The man who has prepared the banquet does not require that his guests change into finer clothes, be healed of their disabilities, or renounce their worldviews and express fidelity to the ideals of their host. He sets a table, then welcomes them to dine. Luke 14 provides a hopeful vision in which those who are unworthy are made worthy, and in which those with power and privilege require no expectations other than that people come as they are.

Note that the man also does not demand that his guests admit their sins or reconcile their pasts before sitting at the table. This piece of the story is often overlooked, because we want so badly for people to be made perfect before they are allowed access to God's goodness. Our religious narratives demand as much—that once we have been allowed to dine with Jesus, we are "made white as snow." Scripture seems explicit in stating that there are no caveats for those who accept the invitation, and that they are to dine from God's abundant table no matter who they are.

In *Just Mercy*, Bryan Stevenson's phenomenal book about the U.S. justice system and its appalling lack of justice for those who are black or poor or both, he notes that "we allow fear, anger, and distance to shape the way we treat the most vulnerable among us."[4] Instead of creating just policies that might help rehabilitate people, our cultural language "reduce[s] people to their worst acts"; we call them drug dealers, thieves, murderers, the criminally insane.[5] By using language that is not in any way person-first, this reductionism drives policies that diminish those accused of crimes, implying that they are not worthy of grace, mercy, humane treatment—and, ultimately, that they are not worthy of justice. Of course there is evil in the world. People act in ways that separate themselves from others and from God. People commit crimes, with devastating consequences. But Jesus makes clear that even those people are not outside the reach of justice and mercy, and that we who are his hands and feet must extend our love to others, however uncomfortable it might be to do so. We are to invite them to the table, to a community that lets them know they are indeed worthy of the invitation and that they will not be left alone. Even when doing so makes us exceedingly uncomfortable. Especially when it does.

Think again about the Luke 14 parable. Who ends up on the wrong side of the story? Certainly not those we might consider unworthy, the ones tracked down by servants and invited at the last minute. No, those whom Jesus condemns in the story are the privileged and powerful who refuse, because of their own interests, the opportunity to commune with others. What if we saw sin in a similar light—not as a list of prohibitions, but as a rejection of community, right relationship, and love? What if we used language that acknowledges we are all image-bearers of God, rather than defining people as sinners and, in the words of Stevenson, reducing them to their worst acts?

The Bible does describe people by their behaviors, noting that there are sinners and tax collectors whom Jesus sits with rather than rejects. Still, Jesus' very act of reaching out to these folks changes who they are; they are not condemned for these identities, but embraced. Jesus' judgment turns instead to those who choose self-interest over others; to those who include the wealthy and ignore the poor crying at their gates; those whose piety and self-righteousness makes them blind, driven by the rule of law rather than grace; those who collude with the powerful. By his very life, his willingness to commune with "sinners and tax collectors," Jesus is affirming the importance of relationship with others, showing that no one, no matter who they are or what they do, is beyond the reach of his friendship, his grace. It is through right relationship with each other—and with Jesus—that we become fully who God means us to be.

Nothing more or nothing less.

AS SOMEONE WHO GREW UP IN THE CHURCH, my Sunday school instruction and the songs we learned helped me imagine heaven as a city paved with gold. As a beautiful mansion with elaborate furnishings and a throne room where God the King would sit beside his Son, the Prince. As fluffy clouds where we could perch, playing harps and singing praise songs to Jesus. That vision no longer has appeal for me, if it ever did, and I'm even less enchanted by the idea that I might be strumming a golden guitar in heaven while those who never uttered the Sinner's Prayer are eternally suffering in the fiery pit of hell.

The great banquet story offers a far more inviting vision of heaven, one where people celebrate their diversity through the unifying act of dining together. It's easy to imagine myself at that kind of table, experiencing the love and validation of beautiful people, celebrating together. Perhaps I like that vision because I've experienced something very much like that here on earth at a sweet sixteen party, when I was forty-six and friends from all walks of life turned my mourning into joy, reminding me that I was worthy. In that moment, they were Jesus to me, and I was transformed. That's the kind of redemptive power Jesus has, letting us know through the amazing grace of others that we are worthy.

12

THE PROMISE OF EXPECTATION

Two years after Ron and I adopted our first son, Benjamin, we decided to add another child to our family, and put our name on an adoption agency waitlist for a boy from India. After four months, we were shown a picture of Saurabh, staring at us mournfully, wearing an orange T-shirt with a cartoon drawing on it that said "Lil' Alligator." This, we knew immediately, was our son. Eighteen months old. Barely standing. A troubling medical history. A cerebral palsy diagnosis. But. Still. We said yes to Saurabh in India, and began to wait.

Our agency promised six to eight months until we could travel to meet him—a length of time that felt bearable, but only barely. Eight months slipped into a year because of agency error, orphanage problems, the Indian government. Over and over, I replayed the three-minute video of a son I hadn't met, mourning a year together we did not have. Watching that video became an incantation of sorts, a ritual of prayer. Please God, be with that boy there, the one kicking the ball, and hitting his friend, and hamming for the camera. Please make something happen so that we might know our son. Not my will, but yours, I wanted to add. But could not.

Several more months passed.

Finally, news: our adoption had cleared its first hurdle in India, and the process could grind forward. Then that summer, in 2005, our wait for Saurabh was further delayed: first by a month-long closure of the Indian courts that made hearing our case impossible; then, only days before we were to travel, a record-breaking monsoon in Mumbai forced us to cancel our trip. But also killed thousands, leaving even more homeless. Please God, I prayed through disappointment, give me perspective.

And then, twenty months after first seeing Saurabh's picture and over two years after signing with an agency, our longest wait was over. We first held Saurabh on a sultry Mumbai morning on the grounds of the Bal Asha orphanage, where he'd spent most of his life. It was immediately clear our son had not been waiting for us. Saurabh spent his last morning at the orphanage sobbing, wiggling out of my arms, crying for his caregivers to save him from the big white folks who had come to take him away. His grief was overwhelming, and I cried while I held him, not sure how to alleviate his suffering and sadness. Over the course of our stay in India to process paperwork, Samuel began the difficult task of attaching to his new parents, although I remember that week—and the fifteen-hour plane ride home—as the most exhausting time of my life. I imagine Samuel, if he could remember that period of his life, might feel the same.

During our two-year wait, people kept telling me that the moment I held my son, I would immediately forget the deep sorrow that accompanied our yearning for Samuel, the sense that time was passing—that our son was growing older without us. Yet our wait was so long, and so painful, so filled with anxiety and mystery and sadness, I knew I would not forget, even as I cradled my boy for the first time. This expanse without Samuel would be part of his own life story, and part of our family's narrative as well.

Samuel is fifteen now, and can grow a full beard. He is a swift runner, a skilled soccer midfielder, a charismatic leader who draws others to him because of his kindness, energy, and good humor. Even still, I often think about the first years of his life, alone in an orphanage that housed eighty other kids. I think about the hope we had in our waiting, and the sadness. I think about the joy of holding Samuel for the first time, a joy mitigated by his fear and loss. I think of the tremendous gift it has been to be his mom, and Benjamin's too: a gift I never expected would feel so immense, so incredible.

When I think about expectation, I think also about the longing we experienced as we waited for Samuel, and about how that expectation was fulfilled, in ways we could not anticipate. It's easy to see the idea of expectation as a negative concept, and to believe we will never live up to expectations telling us exactly who or what we should be. Often, expectation has for me a negative connotation, because of the ways expectations have boxed me in, attempted to define me, made me feel less worthy when expectation has not been met. Expectations have been conveyed to me as biblical truths, without any acknowledgment that the Bible's truths are rarely clear to us, or as "what God wants for you," without any affirmation that sometimes, what God wants for me is frustratingly opaque.

And yet we cannot read the Bible without noting another kind of expectation: the one on which the entire biblical narrative turns. The one that finally offers us freedom from expectation rather than limitation. The one that tells us our expectation for a Messiah has been fulfilled, not by a powerful king come to rule with a mighty hand, but by a poor baby, born in a humble manger stall.

AS PART OF OUR FAITH JOURNEY, we who are Christians contemplate the idea of expectation and what it means for light to break through our darkness, transforming everything. We sing carols about this expectation at Christmas, about our deep yearning for deliverance from suffering and pain, for the long-expected Emmanuel to be born and save us. We light candles and pray and wait through winter nights that stretch out before us, cold and bleak. We think about Mary and what it must have been like for her, an expectant mother, walking to Bethlehem in the last days of her pregnancy.

I don't know exactly what Mary felt, making her way on the road from Nazareth, the pain of labor and delivery looming large before her. But I do know what it means to expect a child with intense longing, and what it means to wait with expectation, filled with hope that your baby will come, and quickly.

The story in Luke 1, narrating the angel's announcement of Jesus' birth to Mary, begins each year's Advent season of waiting. As we wait, we recognize our need for God to rescue us from what enslaves us. The angel's announcement to Mary breathes hope and expectation into that need and reaches across the dark December days until the celebration of Jesus' birth.

I imagine that Mary, filled with longing and expectation, felt the same joy in holding her son for the first time, of getting to be his mother, despite her circumstances. Surely she must have shared some of the frustrations that follow such expectation: sleepless nights, a swiftly mobile baby getting into all manner of trouble, the irritation of a child who won't stop asking existential questions. And also, later, the challenge of watching her son be reviled, sentenced to death because he unsettled the powerful, because he wouldn't bend to the other kind of expectation, the kind telling him exactly who and what he should be as a Jew, a working man, a prophet, a messiah.

While we wait with expectation for the coming of Jesus, we are waiting not only for a small baby in a manger, but for someone who challenged expectations about those with power and prestige. We are waiting for one who repudiated piety and self-righteousness, who called out religious leaders for their rigid adherence to the law, who dined with outcasts and sought followers among the poor. In his life and his ministry, Jesus not only elevated the marginalized in his culture, but also became an outcast himself, a reminder that even those among us deemed unworthy by our culture reflect the image of God, just as they are.

In Luke 1, Mary's song reminds us of the role to which she was called, one that elevates the poor and strikes down the powerful. Upon hearing from an angel that she is to give birth, Mary praises a God who "has brought down rulers from their thrones but has lifted up the humble. He has filled the hungry with good things but has sent the rich away empty" (Luke 1:52-53 NIV). Those anticipating the prophets' assurance that a king would save Israel could not accept this vision of leadership, one strong on humility, grace, and mercy. The son for whom Mary waits with expectation will come to change the world completely by being who God created him to be, even though the world was expecting someone else entirely.

This is the person our own waiting celebrates. This is the one who reminds us we are worthy. When we hear countless messages telling us to be, do, and think differently, this is the one who tells us there are only two expectations that matter: to love God with all your heart, soul, and mind, and to love your neighbor as yourself. Our lives should be a living testimony to these expectations, a reminder that every person—yes, *every last one*—is a beautiful, wonderful image-bearer of the divine.

ONE OF MY ALL-TIME FAVORITE HYMNS is "Come, Thou Long-Expected Jesus." In the church calendar, we sing the hymn mostly during Advent. But the song names our deep longing to be freed from the tyranny of the world we now live in, every day of the year. Written in the mid-1700s by Charles Wesley, the song was originally inspired by Wesley's concern for the economic disparity he saw around him. Although it lacks the buoyancy of other Christmas carols—think "Joy to the World" and "O Come, All Ye Faithful"—the hymn accurately reflects the desperation of Advent's waiting, and the hope that a Messiah might soon arrive to save us. The song's first stanza tells us our hope is in the arrival of Jesus, who breaks in to the world to save us from our fear and sin; and the second stanza reminds us that Jesus confounds our expectations, arriving as a child and a king. We sing this hymn during Advent not only to mark Jesus' birth but to remember that we still have a deep longing, one that will only be fulfilled when it is Jesus—rather than our sins and our fears—who alone rules us.

While some Christians might think this song anticipates the second coming of Jesus, I'm drawn to these lyrics because they show me what might be possible here, on earth, in our time. Rather than looking forward to the moment when we are "raised" to God's "glorious throne," the song challenges me to consider how Jesus' love for all and the care with which he related to the least of these can reign within us, can in itself free us from the fears and sins that ensnare us. What do I do in my daily life to make sure I treat others as Jesus would call me to? How do I ensure that I am making others know that they are worthy? How do I ask, each moment, for the long-expected Jesus to reign in my life?

And what does it mean, really, to ask Jesus to "rule in all our hearts alone"? Because our Christian narratives so often point to the Big Jesus Moment, we might assume that once we've said the simple Jesus prayer inviting him into our hearts, we are set: a one-and-done deal that seals our eternity in the afterlife. But Jesus saves us in a far more immediate and profound way when we recognize how Jesus' love for us—and our love for each other—creates the world Jesus calls us to, one that replicates heaven here on earth. In a way, we wait with expectation for Jesus because Jesus delivers us from expectation, his life and ministry reminding us that we are all worthy, simply because we all wholly reflect the image of our Creator. We are called to that recognition, too, seeing people as exactly who they were created to be in a world insisting they be someone else entirely. And once we do this—once we love others enough to allow them to be just as they are—we experience the saving grace of understanding finally what it means to know and extend God's unconditional love.

THE ADVENT SEASON I REMEMBER BEST was the one that occurred four months after we brought Samuel home. For the first time, I understood more fully what Advent meant because I understood what expectation meant. Our first adoption had gone so smoothly, and I didn't have time to experience the same expectation that I later did with Samuel, whose homecoming took so long. I had never desired something more in my life than having Samuel home with us. Yet in the months after his arrival, I never felt more acutely the expectation to be someone I could not be.

Samuel was frenetic then, rolling through our house, his heart and mind on sensory overload. After spending his lifetime in an orphanage, he was making up for everything he missed: touching, climbing, pushing, swinging, jumping, dancing, crying. But not sleeping. Not much. I was exhausted, trying to be the mom he needed me to be, and helping Benjamin adjust, too, to this bundle of fury sharing his life.

On a particularly overwhelming Saturday morning close to Christmas, a bookstore story time descended into chaos. Samuel was running through the aisle flinging clothes off his body, and while I was chasing him, Benjamin was expelled from the story circle for talking because another kid kicked him in the back. I drove both boys home, sweat-drenched and crying, raging at the injustice of Benjamin's expulsion and my ineffectual parenting.

"I think we made a huge mistake," I sobbed to my husband when I got home. "We shouldn't have adopted again." Ron pulled me in, hugged me tight, and told me that things would get better and that Samuel was supposed to be part of our family.

He was right. But weeks before Christmas, and with the threat of Samuel's removal from our little Christian preschool because he couldn't always follow rules about sitting quietly (he didn't know much English, but this didn't matter!), I felt the winter's darkness closing in, the expectations to be a better mom, to have a better family, overwhelming. I needed someone to have faith in me and in my son so that I could have faith that the light we were expecting would come, would deliver us from loneliness and pain.

On Christmas Eve, we took the boys to our church's candlelight service. The children's pastor stopped us at the door, wondering if we could help her during the processional, when the figures in the nativity were brought forward and placed in the crèche. Maybe someone hadn't shown up that night and she was desperate for help; maybe she'd planned to ask us all along; maybe God spoke to her in the moment—for whatever reason, Pastor Michelle had seen my son as more than the troublemaker who climbed on tables and spoke inexplicable phrases. She had entrusted him with a role in the Christmas story, the most important narrative of our faith, one not about a Big Jesus coming down to convert us all but about a helpless infant, born in an unexpected place and meant to save us.

A little later, as I watched from the balcony, my husband walked down the center aisle of the crowded church, holding hands with each son. Benjamin skipped and Samuel ran beside him, trying to keep up with Ron's long stride. At the crèche, Ron and our sons situated wise man statues next to the manger, the whole nativity knocked askew by our sons' small hands. And there the holy family stood with shepherds and kings and donkeys—seeming a little crazed, a little off-center—waiting for their world to be changed.

After placing the figurines in the nativity, Samuel climbed on my lap and nestled against my chest. He sat silently for the remaining service, listening to Scripture, humming along to carols. When the homily finally ended, he cupped his hand in mine to receive a lighted candle from his father. Samuel's brown eyes glinted bright in the flame, witness to this ritual of fire in church and of light glowing in the darkened sanctuary. As I sang "Silent Night" into the nape of Samuel's neck, I sighed at the miracle of my newest son.

Our expectation was answered, and we were—all of us—transformed.

ACKNOWLEDGMENTS

Writing a book like this one has allowed me to see with new clarity the many people throughout my life who affirmed me, who encouraged my vocational calling, and who let me know I am a worthy image-bearer of God. I am extraordinarily grateful for those countless others whose affirmation made me who I am today, and I am wary, too, knowing that I might forget to acknowledge people whose behind-the-scenes efforts have made this book possible.

I am grateful to George Fox University for a semester's sabbatical to work on this project, and for granting me the great privilege of space to read, write, and think. George Fox is an amazing institution, in large part because of its students, many of whom have made me a better person through their time in my classes. If I listed every student who has influenced my life, I might go on for pages, but you all know who you are, and I am thankful for the four (more or less) years we spent together. In particular, I am grateful that Heather Harney and Julia Howell agreed to read my manuscript and provide honest feedback, just when I needed it most.

Also, my colleagues in the English department make coming to work a delight, and I'm grateful for their continued encouragement, especially my chair, Gary Tandy, who overcame his evangelical haircut to become a spiritual mentor to me; and Polly Peterson, whose shared love for the B students in the world has enriched my own teaching in innumerable ways.

Because I was a B student myself, I am grateful for early teachers who saw something in me that I couldn't see myself. Karin Krakauer, my first high school English teacher, made me think I could be a writer, and Ed Higgins and Becky Ankeny at George Fox College made me think I could be a scholar. My master's thesis advisor at the University of Missouri-St. Louis, Sally Ebest, made me believe I could be a teacher, and fostered the skills to start me on that journey. This book reflects many of the ideas these folks taught me about writing and about life.

Being a writer is by turns exhilarating and demoralizing, and thus I am grateful for those who have supported my written endeavors, despite my vacillating moods. Thanks to Valerie Weaver-Zercher and Amy Gingerich at Herald Press, who helped shape my vision for this book and who have been excellent editors. The influence of my writing partner, Kendra Weddle Irons, is everywhere in this book, and I am thankful for the many, many ways Kendra has been a friend, ally, and mentor to me.

I have lived in the Newberg, Oregon, area for twenty years, and my love for the people here is immense, including those who have provided pastoral care: Gregg Koskela, Elizabeth Sherwood, and Leslie Murray. Their sermons came at just the right time, informing what I was trying (and often failing) to write. They have taught me what a thoughtful, loving faith looks like, and I am grateful for their influence. Thank you as well to my brainy Bible study group—Jill Jamison Beals, Heidi Hopkins, and Kim Steffen—whose questions about atonement theology especially (and about Jesus donuts too) have helped shape my faith perspective for this second half of my life.

My mother-runner friends in Newberg have been invaluable in my processing for this book, and many of the ideas expressed here started from conversations we had together out on the road, putting in our miles. I am grateful for Staci Llieuallen's thoughtful perspective on Christian culture, and for Kimberly Doades's unabashed, constant encouragement, especially as an outsider to evangelicalism. And I am especially thankful for Leslie Brittell, who has taught me so much about so many things in our four years as best friends, running and otherwise; my life is far richer, and this book far better, because Leslie took the risk to write me a Facebook message in February 2014, asking me if I wanted to go for a run.

Finally, I somehow managed to luck out by having the best family ever, and their encouragement, love, and grace is threaded through these pages. I'm thankful for my parents, Esther and Ed Springer, who nurtured me into being exactly who God created me to be, and for my brother, Todd Springer, who keeps me honest, and who always thinks I can do more than I believe I can, especially where mountain biking is concerned. Ever since we changed from bitter enemies to best friends in high school, my sister, Amy Landes, has been my biggest cheerleader, and I am thankful for her willingness to read this book in draft form; no one knows me better than my sister does, and yet, despite this, she loves me fiercely. I am a far better person because of her.

My husband has always taken the brunt of my writer's angst, and his patience and care throughout my sabbatical, especially in light of his own stress and sadness after his dad's death, helped me meet my deadlines (and he knows how important those deadlines are to me!). Moment by moment, I am grateful for him and the family we've created together, including my stepchildren, Melissa and Ryan, who have become really cool adults to converse with about almost anything; and my sons, Benjamin and Samuel, who have made my life infinitely better. Seeing them grow into amazing young men has been a delight, and I know they are well on their way to becoming exactly who God created them to be.

NOTES

INTRODUCTION

1. See, for example, Donna Partow's *Becoming the Woman God Wants Me to Be: A 90-Day Guide to Living the Proverbs 31 Life* (Grand Rapids, MI: Revell, 2008). Partow provides advice about financial planning, diet, and clothing choices that will ideally help a reader become a "Proverbs 31 woman."

1. THIS IS THE WORLD WE LIVE IN

1. Letha Dawson Scanzoni and Nancy Hardesty, *All We're Meant to Be: Biblical Feminism for Today*, 2nd ed. (Nashville: Abingdon, 1986). First edition published 1974.
2. "John McArthur on How to Respond to a Homosexual Child," Grace to You, June 3, 2014, video, 1:54, https://www.gty.org/library/blog/B140603/john-macarthur-on-how-to-respond-to-a-homosexual-child.

2. WHEN BIG JESUS DOESN'T SHOW UP

1. Madeleine L'Engle, *The Rock That Is Higher: Story as Truth* (Wheaton, IL: Harold Shaw, 1993), 215.
2. Daniel Burke, "The Dirty Little Secret about Religious Conversion Stories," CNN, November 11, 2015, http://www.cnn.com/2015/11/10/politics/carson-religious-conversion/index.html.

3. John Pavlovitz, "The Bible Belt Needs Jesus," *John Pavlovitz: Stuff That Needs to Be Said* (blog), January 4, 2017, https://johnpavlovitz.com/2017/01/04/conservative-white-christians-need-jesus/.

4. Bret Lott, "Toward a Definition of Creative Nonfiction," in Robert L. Root Jr. and Michael J. Steinberg, *The Fourth Genre: Contemporary Writers of/on Creative Nonfiction*, 3rd ed. (Upper Saddle River, NJ: Pearson, 2005), 361.

3. STICKY FAITH OR BEING STUCK?

1. Michael Lipka, "Millennials Increasingly Are Driving Growth of 'Nones,'" Pew Research Center, May 12, 2015, http://www.pewresearch.org/fact-tank/2015/05/12/millennials-increasingly-are-driving-growth-of-nones/.

2. See, for example, Rachel Held Evans, "Want Millennials Back in the Pews? Stop Trying to Make Church 'Cool,'" *Washington Post*, April 30, 2015, https://www.washington post.com/opinions/jesus-doesnt-tweet/2015/04/30/fb07ef1a-ed01-11e4-8666-a1d756d0218e_story.html. Evans analyzes several recent polls about religion in America, convincingly arguing that young people are looking for an authentic expression of faith, one that acknowledges brokenness and doubt and is inclusive in its reach.

3. Rachel Held Evans, "Why Millennials Are Leaving the Church," *CNN Belief Blog*, July 27, 2013, http://religion.blogs.cnn.com/2013/07/27/why-millennials-are-leaving-the-church/.

4. Kara E. Powell and Chap Clark, *Sticky Faith: Everyday Ideas to Build Lasting Faith in Your Kids* (Grand Rapids, MI: Zondervan, 2011).

4. THERE'S A PROBLEM WITH YOU GUYS

1. Greg Lukianoff and Jonathan Haidt, "The Coddling of the American Mind," *The Atlantic*, September 2015, https://www.theatlantic.com/magazine/archive/2015/09/the-coddling-of-the-american-mind/399356/.

2. Lera Boroditsky, "How Does Our Language Shape the Way We Think?," Edge, June 11, 2009, https://www.edge.org/ conversation/lera_boroditsky-how-does-our-language-shape-the-way-we-think.

3. "Why Pledge," R-Word (website), accessed November 7, 2017, http://www.r-word.org/r-word-why-pledge.aspx# .WgItLHa1thE.

4. Parker J. Palmer, "The Risk of Incarnation: A Christmas Meditation," *On Being* (blog), December 24, 2014, https:// onbeing.org/blog/the-risk-of-incarnation-a-christmas-meditation/.

5. Ibid.

6. Jeanne Murray Walker, "Is It Possible to Read and Write in a Post-Factual World?," From the Desk of Jeanne Murray Walker email newsletter, December 14, 2016, http://us7 .campaign-archive2.com/?u=3e62f03708ae64c114f2a8b7 b&id=a4d75a8cbd.

7. Doug Frank, *A Gentler God: Breaking Free of the Almighty in the Company of a Human Jesus* (Menangle, Australia: Albatross Books, 2010).

8. Virginia Ramey Mollenkott, "2017 Mother Eagle Award Recipient," recorded acceptance speech, Gay Christian Network Conference, January 5, 2017, Pittsburgh, PA, 10:10, https://youtu.be/uAMpzmMqrmk.

9. Mary Daly, *Beyond God the Father: Toward a Philosophy of Women's Liberation* (Boston: Beacon, 1973).

5. SEARCHING FOR THE GOOD LIFE

1. See "Singles Now Outnumber Marrieds in America, and That's a Good Thing," Public Radio International: The Takeaway, September 14, 2014, https://www.pri.org/ stories/2014-09-14/singles-now-outnumber-married-people-america-and-thats-good-thing; and "Census 2016: More Canadians Than Ever are Living Alone, and Other Take-aways," *The Globe and Mail*, August 2, 2017, https://www .theglobeandmail.com/news/national/census-2016-statscan/ article35861448/.

2. Rebecca Adams, "If You Feel Bad about Being Single, It's Not Because You're Single," Huffington Post, May 29, 2014, https://www.huffingtonpost.com/2014/05/01/being-single-happiness-women_n_5007469.html.

3. Bella DePauto, "23 Ways Single People Are Better: The Scientific Evidence," *Psychology Today*, May 4, 2014, https://www.psychologytoday.com/blog/living-single/201405/23-ways-single-people-are-better-the-scientific-evidence.

4. John Blake, "Why Young Christians Aren't Waiting Anymore," CNN, September 27, 2011, http://religion.blogs.cnn.com/2011/09/27/why-young-christians-arent-waiting-anymore/.

5. Keven Lui, "This Is How Much It Costs to Get Married in the U.S. on Average," *Fortune Magazine*, February 3, 2017, http://fortune.com/2017/02/03/wedding-cost-spending-usa-average/.

6. In *Real Marriage*, for example, the Driscolls answer questions about cosmetic surgery by taking such considerations through a rubric: Is it lawful? Is it helpful? Is it enslaving? They conclude that cosmetic surgery "can make us more attractive to our spouses. And if our appearance is improved, we feel more comfortable being seen naked by our spouses, which can increase our freedom in lovemaking." Grace Driscoll and Mark Driscoll, *Real Marriage: The Truth about Sex, Friendship, and Life Together* (Nashville: Thomas Nelson, 2013), 199.

7. Quoted in Katherine Weber, "Pat Robertson Suggests 'Awful Looking' Women Can Ruin Marriages," *Christian Post*, January 14, 2013, https://www.christianpost.com/news/pat-robertson-suggests-awful-looking-women-can-ruin-marriages-88245/.

8. Alina Tugend, "Childless Women to Marketers: We Buy Stuff Too," *New York Times*, July 9, 2016, https://www.nytimes.com/2016/07/10/business/childless-women-to-marketers-we-buy-things-too.html?.

9. Kathleen Nielson, "The Problem with a Childfree Life," The Gospel Coalition, August 7, 2013, https://www.thegospel coalition.org/article/the-problem-with-the-childfree-life/.

10. See, for example, Thai Nguyen, "10 Important Reasons to Start Making Time for Silence, Rest and Solitude," Huffington Post, November 3, 2014, https://www.huffingtonpost .com/thai-nguyen/10-important-reasons-to-s_b_6035662 .html. Nguyen curates several studies detailing the significant psychological and physiological benefits of making space for silence and solitude.

11. Anne Lamott, *Traveling Mercies: Some Thoughts on Faith* (New York: Anchor, 1999), 168–69.

6. WHY MOWING THE LAWN CAN BE COMPLICATED

1. Nedra Pickler, "White House Promotes Economic Issues Facing Women," *San Diego Union Tribune*, March 12, 2014, http://www.sandiegouniontribune.com/sdut-white-house-promotes-economic-issues-facing-women-2014mar12-story.html.

2. Allie Bidwell, "Women More Likely to Graduate College, but Still Earn Less Than Men," *U.S. World and News Report*, October 31, 2014, https://www.usnews.com/news/ blogs/data-mine/2014/10/31/women-more-likely-to-graduate-college-but-still-earn-less-than-men.

3. Katie Zezima and Philip Rucker, "Trump on How Women Should Deal with Harassment," *Washington Post*, August 2, 2016, https://www.washingtonpost.com/politics/donald-and-eric-trump-opine-on-sexual-harassment--and-draw-fire/2016/08/02/9814549e-58c5-11e6-9aee-8075993d73a2_ story.html?utm_term=.9b973a61a1de.

4. In *If Eve Only Knew*, a book I cowrote with Kendra Weddle Irons, we address this phenomena in a chapter called "What Happens in the Silence." Kendra Weddle Irons and Melodie Springer Mock, *If Eve Only Knew: Freeing Yourself from Biblical Womanhood and Becoming All God Means for You to Be* (St. Louis: Chalice Press, 2015), 131–54.

5. Ed Yong, "6-Year-Old Girls Already Have Gendered Beliefs about Intelligence," *The Atlantic*, January 26, 2017, https://www.theatlantic.com/science/archive/2017/01/six-year-old-girls-already-have-gendered-beliefs-about-intelligence/514340/.

7. HAIR (AND A THIGH GAP) MAKES A GIRL

1. Carolyn Coker Ross, "Why Do Women Hate Their Bodies?" *World of Psychology* (blog), June 2, 2012, https://psychcentral.com/blog/archives/2012/06/02/why-do-women-hate-their-bodies/.

2. Anne Lamott, *Traveling Mercies: Some Thoughts on Faith* (New York: Anchor, 1999), 173–74.

3. Amanda Scherker, "7 Ways the Beauty Industry Convinced Women They Weren't Good Enough," Huffington Post, April 29, 2015, https://www.huffingtonpost.com/2014/04/29/beauty-industry-women_n_5127078.html.

4. Lindy West, *Shrill: Notes from a Loud Woman* (New York: Hatchette, 2016), 67–68.

5. University of North Carolina at Chapel Hill, "Three out of Four Women Have Disordered Eating, Survey Suggests," ScienceDaily, April 23, 2008, https://www.sciencedaily.com/releases/2008/04/080422202514.htm.

6. Nancy LeTourneau, "What the 60-Billion-Dollar Weight Loss Industry Doesn't Want You to Know," *Washington Monthly*, May 2, 2016, https://washingtonmonthly.com/2016/05/02/what-the-60-billion-weight-loss-industry-doesnt-want-you-to-know/.

7. Tim Challies, "Letting Herself Go," Challies (website), May 26, 2011, https://www.challies.com/christian-living/letting-herself-go/.

8. Amy Joy, "Allowing Yourself to Be Feminine," *Corner of Joy* (blog), June 26, 2012, http://cornerofjoy.blogspot.com/2012/06/allowing-yourself-to-be-feminine.html.

9. Darcy Lagana, "How God Got a Tomboy to Embrace Her Femininity," *Charisma*, April 4, 2014, https://www.charismamag.com/life/women/20274-how-god-got-a-tomboy-to-embrace-her-femininity.

10. "High Rates of Suicide and Self-Harm Among Transgender Youth," *Science Daily*, August 31, 2016. https://www.sciencedaily.com/releases/2016/08/160831110833.htm.

11. Nick Bilton, "Parenting in the Age of Online Pornography," *New York Times*, January 7, 2015, https://www.nytimes.com/2015/01/08/style/parenting-in-the-age-of-online-porn.html.

12. Quoted in Char Adams, "Women's Bodies Don't Exist for Public Consumption," *People*, August 13, 2015, http://people.com/celebrity/kiran-gandhi-period-runner-speaks-out-against-critics/.

13. Sharon Hodde Miller, "How 'Modest Is Hottest' Is Hurting Christian Women," *Christianity Today*, December 15, 2011, http://www.christianitytoday.com/women/2011/december/how-modest-is-hottest-is-hurting-christian-women.html.

14. Study quoted in David Briggs, "This Is My Body: How Christian Theology Affects Body Image," *Christianity Today*, October 26, 2016, http://www.christianitytoday.com/news/2016/october/how-christian-theology-affects-body-image-body-shaming.html.

8. WHAT'S THE MATTER WITH BEING BLESSED

1. Quoted in Albert Mohler, "The Osteen Predicament: Mere Happiness Cannot Bear the Weight of the Gospel," Albert Mohler (website), September 3, 2014, http://www.albertmohler.com/2014/09/03/the-osteen-predicament-mere-happiness-cannot-bear-the-weight-of-the-gospel/.

2. Cathleen Falsani, "The Prosperity Gospel," *Washington Post*, December 2009, http://www.washingtonpost.com/wp-srv/special/opinions/outlook/worst-ideas/prosperity-gospel.html.

3. Jessica Bennett, "They Feel 'Blessed': Blessed Becomes a Popular Hashtag on Social Media," *New York Times*, May 2, 2014, https://www.nytimes.com/2014/05/04/fashion/blessed-becomes-popular-word-hashtag-social-media.html.

4. "God's Purpose for Your Life," In Touch Ministries (website), March 18, 2015, https://www.intouch.org/read/gods-purpose-for-your-life.

5. Jessica Kelley, *Lord Willing? Wrestling with God's Role in My Child's Death* (Harrisonburg, VA: Herald Press, 2016), 60.

9. THE CHURCH'S PROBLEM WITH THE BIG BUT

1. Bob Jones Sr., "Is Segregation Scriptural?," sermon, Bob Jones University, April 17, 1960, Greenville, SC, radio broadcast. A transcript is available at Camille Lewis, "'Is Segregation Scriptural?' by Bob Jones Sr, 1960," A Time to Laugh, March 15, 2013, http://www.drslewis.org/camille/2013/03/15/is-segregation-scriptural-by-bob-jones-sr-1960/.
2. Ibid.
3. Gregg Koskela, "Honest Thoughts," *Out of Doubt* (blog), May 10, 2017, https://outofdoubt.wordpress.com/2017/05/10/honest-thoughts/.

10. CHALLENGING MESSAGES AND CHANGING THE WORLD

1. At one time, *World Magazine* included "biblical objectivity" as one part of its mission. Marvin Olasky, editor in chief for *World Magazine*, defined biblical objectivity in his 1996 book, *Telling the Truth: How to Revitalize Christian Journalism*. Olasky's *Telling the Truth* can be found at https://www.worldmag.com/world/olasky/truthc1.html.
2. Kendra Weddle Irons and Melanie Springer Mock, *If Eve Only Knew: Freeing Yourself from Biblical Womanhood and Becoming All God Means for You to Be* (St. Louis: Chalice Press, 2015), 105.
3. Stephen Mattson, "Exploiting Scripture in the Name of Jesus," *Sojourners*, March 24, 2017, https://sojo.net/articles/exploiting-scripture-name-jesus.
4. Roxane Gay, *Bad Feminist* (New York: Harper Collins, 2014), 168.
5. Ibid.

11. REDEEMING A NOT-SO-SWEET SIXTEENTH

1. Sheryl Sandberg and Adam Grant, *Option B: Facing Adversity, Building Resilience, Finding Joy* (New York: Knopf, 2017), 133.
2. Ibid., 134.
3. John Moe, "Placebo: A Conversation with Ana Marie Cox," May 5, 2017, in *The Hilarious World of Depression*, podcast, 1:20:08, https://www.apmpodcasts.org/thwod/2017/05/a-conversation-with-ana-marie-cox/.
4. Bryan Stevenson, *Just Mercy: A Story of Justice and Redemption* (New York: Spiegel and Grau, 2014), 14.
5. Ibid., 15.

THE AUTHOR

Melanie Springer Mock is a professor
of English at George Fox University
and the author or editor of five books,
including *If Eve Only Knew*. Her essays
and reviews have appeared in *The
Nation*, *Chronicle of Higher Education*,
Christian Feminism Today, Literary
Mama, and *Christianity Today*, among
others. She and her husband and sons live in Dundee, Oregon.